AW WITH WORDS

Young Writers' 16th Annual Poetry Competition

It is feeling and force of imagination that make us eloquent.

How can I not dream while writing? The blank page gives a right to dream.

Young**Writers**

Around The UK

Edited by Heather Killingray

 Young**Writers**

First published in Great Britain in 2007 by:
Young Writers
Remus House
Coltsfoot Drive
Peterborough
PE2 9JX
Telephone: 01733 890066
Website: www.youngwriters.co.uk

SB ISBN 978-1 84431 201 6

Foreword

This year, the Young Writers' *Away With Words* competition proudly presents a showcase of the best poetic talent selected from thousands of up-and-coming writers nationwide.

Young Writers was established in 1991 to promote the reading and writing of poetry within schools and to the young of today. Our books nurture and inspire confidence in the ability of young writers and provide a snapshot of poems written in schools and at home by budding poets of the future.

The thought, effort, imagination and hard work put into each poem impressed us all and the task of selecting poems was a difficult but nevertheless enjoyable experience.

We hope you are as pleased as we are with the final selection and that you and your family continue to be entertained with *Away With Words Around The UK* for many years to come.

Contents

Chelsie Harrison (12)   30
Josh Gardner (11)   30
Lucy Richardson (11)   31
Elizabeth Power (12)   31
Thomas Chard (12)   32
Megan McCarter (11)   32
Matthew Gardner (11)   33
Jenny Turner (11)   33
Heather Allen (11)   34
Richard Radcliffe (11)   34
James Harrison (11)   35
Breeshey Mort (12)   35
Alex Maitland (11)   36
Jade Booth (11)   37
Fraser Veale (11)   37
Kelly Firth (12)   38
Ellie Harrison (12)   38

Chace Community School, Enfield
Lisa Sabine (14)   39
Emily Hart (14)   39
Nicola Lewis (14)   40

Copland Community School, Wembley
Miten Hirani (11)   40
Amura Abdullahi (14)   41
Hardik Rohitkumar (12)   41
Azzah ElHabashy (14)   42
Amina Marzouki (14)   42
Zennah Mogul (13)   43
Walid Aimaq (12)   43
Payal Patel (14)   44
Amal Abdi (14)   45
Oltiana Dervishi (11)   46
Rory Eduh (12)   46
Hanaa Ennast Eldrissi (11)   47
Nasrina Hassan (12)   47
Ashish Patel (12)   48
Fayola Mawulawde (11)   48
Shalin Patel (14)   49

Alex Tipping (12) 71
Aled Jones (12) 71
Josh Coulton (12) 72
Rhiannon Sheppard (11) 72
Alex Williams (11) 73
Abigail Sadler (11) 74
Georgia Davies (12) 75
Ruth Cochrane (12) 75
Charlotte Jones (12) 76
Louise Powell (12) 76
Richard Taylor (11) 77
Owen Haslegrave (12) 77
Ryan Price (13) 78
Ned Bramley (12) 78

Lewis School, Pengam, Bargoed

Owen Dare (14) 79
Rhys Owens (14) 80
Alex Williams (14) 81
Nathan Hazell (13) 81
Amar Ali (13) 82
Ben Fussell (16) 83
Liam Shaughnessy (14) 84
Ieuan Protheroe (16) 85
Lee Knicz (13) 86
Ryan Lintern (13) 87
David Shenton (14) 88
James Fletcher (15) 89
Craig Evans (15) 90

Lliswerry High School, Newport

Jack Bradshaw (12) 90
Pritesh Patel (11) 91
Sam Berrecloth (12) 92
Adrienne Harris (11) 93

Maesydderwen Comp School, Ystradynlais

Rhysian Jones (14) 94
Natalie Clare Powell (14) 95

St Cyres School, Penarth

St Illtyd's RC High School, Cardiff

Sybil Elgar School (NAS) Southall

The Ash Technology College, Ashford

Willows High School, Cardiff

Ysgol Bryn Alyn, Wrexham

Ysgol Bryn Elian, Colwyn Bay

The Poems

Five Silver Bullets

The silence is shattered and everyone stares;
The rain begins falling but nobody cares.

A clatter and a splash and the gun comes down
And the high judging city hurts what it found.
Raindrops, streaked red, lash down from the sky,
And nobody thought what had made the kid cry.
Nobody knew where the boy had a home,
Nobody cared that he sat there alone.
Does anyone know that for him there's no sun?
Does anyone care what made him get that gun?
Showed his fake ID to the man at the store,
Took some lives in his hands; what was it for?
Where was his mother the day that he died,
Alone on the streets where nobody cried?
Where'd his daddy go when he fought with his wife
And left the house crying, with a kitchen knife?
What was he thinking as he ran down the street,
As the ground underneath him tore at his feet?
One reigning statement, life's not fair
And they all turn away as they're told not to stare.
Two shots ring out;
Then three;
Then four;
The sound of the rain is the tears on the floor.
He turns the gun on himself, his conscience to mend;
He's somebody's kid; he's nobody's friend.
He died that day, the boy with no name,
Alone on the streets and who is to blame?
In truth, he didn't die there on the floor;
He died when his family walked out the door.

The silence is shattered and everyone stares;
The rain begins falling but nobody cares.

Sarah Millar (14)

Marie Celeste

Though nine men dwell on the Marie
Celeste and lassies gone missing.
It was I, that unfortunate night, that
found the ship afloat. As we steered
through the lee, we caught no
glimmer through the night.

As we neared the ghostly ship
the waves turned to mountains and the
sea was cold as ice. As we got nearer
to the lonely ship we saw the sails of
towering white. The big black, blistered
clouds unleashed some thunder that
nearly tore our boat apart.

As we neared the ghostly ship we were
too amazed to speak. We climbed up
onto the deserted deck with no one in
our sight. There was a strange scent of death; and so
wondering, side by side, we stood for
a moment still tongue-tied.

Hard on each other's heels we passed
into the cabin. Yet as we rushed
through the door we saw a table
which held an untouched meal.

We hunted high, we hunted low, we
hunted from top to bottom and end to
end, just to find a ripped up sail and a
missing lifeboat. Soon we had ransacked
the deserted boat.

Of the eleven people's fate
we found no trace, of any kind,
in any place.

As we listened to the roaring waves
we came to think about its past.
Twelve men missing, three men dead
and one we knew as a friend leapt
from the deck into the sea, down to
the seabed.

Long we thought of what fate would
come to these poor chaps. As we
stood there silently we thought of the
untouched meal, the ripped up sail
and the lifeboat that was still missing.

We seemed to stand for an endless
while and still no word was said,
eleven people alive on the Marie
Celeste, who thought on eleven
people dead.

Ryan Urquhart (12)

Kitten To Cat

Two hours old am I,
Go straight for milk, I don't need to be told how and why.
This world is full of staring eyes, shouts, miaows and cries.
Those first few days were such fun;
Play fights, warm milk and cuddles from Mum.

One by one my brothers and sisters went away.
My owners said they'd keep just one, if that was OK.
But no one brought me back to their home,
So I was left all alone.

As I grew up I learned how to be tough.
On the whole it was quite rough.
Many a kitten of my own I had,
I bet they are glad they had me as their dad.

I took many a mouse and a rat's life,
And my claws grew as sharp as a knife.
But, alas I grew old
And liked the fire better than the cold.
So now my aching bones are dire,
It's time for a last sleep by the fire.

Hannah Pezzack (11)

The Marie Celeste

'Twas a cool, clear day on the ocean blue,
The day we found that ship.
There wasn't even a wind or breeze,
The day we found that ship.
It seemed to be fine, nothing strange,
Just floating on the gentle waves,
There was no noise, no sound at all,
Just floating on the gentle waves.

But as we neared, the sea turned grey,
The sky was a sheet of black.
The vessel seemed to shimmer white,
Like a ghost ship glowing in the night,
Shivers trickled down our backs,
The strange thing is, though it was scary,
Something drew me to that ship,
Though it seemed to shimmer white,
Like a ghost ship in the night,
Something told me not to turn back.

We sailed up beside it, drawn into its gloom,
And crept onto the deck, damp and dark.
We whispered and shouted,
Bellowed and yelled,
But nothing, nothing, answered us back.
Our footsteps creaked on the old wooden floor,
As we searched for signs of life,
The frosty air consumed our breath,
As we searched for signs of life.

All of a sudden an ice-cold wind,
Swept through the ship and through our bones.
Our screams were swallowed by the mist and fog,
Drowned out by the creaking and the groans.
I started to wish I'd stayed away from that ship,
There was something that scared me, something not quite right,
The vessel was almost in perfect condition,
But deserted in the sea, shimmering white.
Like a ghost ship in the night.
Swallowed by mist and fog.

What kind of fate met the crew?
Do their bodies still walk this Earth?
What kind of torture did they bear,
Did they survive the frightful nightmare?
What could have happened? What is the truth?

As we pondered on this puzzle,
A piercing roar shook the ship.
A flash of lightning lit the sky,
I ran for cover but lost my grip.
I was hurled through the air onto my boat,
I lay alone upon the dark, damp deck,
Concealed by the mist and fog.

My heart was pounding,
My head was spinning,
I was wrapped in a blanket of ice.
Screams and cries flowing through my mind,
How to stop them I couldn't find,
As I lay concealed by the mist and fog.

My dreams torment me every night,
Since the day we found that ship,
My life turned upside down,
The day we found that ship . . .

Ben Jones (12)

Rose

The petal of the rose
One of the greatest
Features that God made.

The autumn comes
As the wind blows harder
The leaves fall
And the petal of the rose
Shall fall one day.

Anila Abbas

Trapped

I don't know why I stayed
I could have got away
I didn't need to fall
Just fight back, that's all

You didn't need to hurt me
You could have made me loved
You should have been proud
Not so angry and loud

I can never get those pictures
Out of my head
Of pain and misery
And the feeling of dread

Cold and alone
You kept me that way
Drowning in my sorrow
Every single day

I cried within myself
Feeling nothing but pain
Counting down the hours
Till you hurt me again

What did I do
To deserve your punishment?
I did the best I could
But you would still torment

You always put me down
And told me I was wrong
I can't believe I stayed
With you so long

Now I've broken free
Now I'm looking back
I wonder why I let you
I could have fought right back.

Susan McGarvie (13)

The Hope Of The Heart

Holding hands,
Quick smiles, a glance.
Just about sums up our love.

He betrayed me,
He played me,
And like a bottle of fizzy drink,
He shook my heart around,
Just to the point when it's fit to burst
And just like the fizzy drink,
My love for him will turn flat.

I can't understand why I love him so,
Or why I can't forget him, let it go.
When we meet he is distant,
When we walk together,
There's nothing.
Yet my attraction to him is unstopping,
It hurts so much,
When I know how he plays me.

Or is it just my self-esteem,
My trust?
Does he really love me,
Or was that day just lust?

Oh, I wish,
I wish I could see right through him,
Like all my friends do,
But I can't,
'Cause I hope,
That he may love me too.

Samantha Carr (13)

Horrible Fears

H ippopotomonstrosesquippedaliophobia -
    Fearing long words,
    My biggest fear is the word smiles,
    Work it out it might take a while.

O neirophobia -
    Evil puppets ripping by the seams,
    All in my scary dreams.

R adiophobia -
    Fearing X-rays,
    The bright blue light makes me daze
    Every time I have X-rays.

R anidaphobia -
    Fearing frogs,
    Big, fat slimy toads,
    Dead and flat on a long stretched road.

I chthyophobia -
    Fearing fish,
    Big sloppy fish,
    Clear him off the dish!

B rontophobia -
    Fearing thunder,
    Thumping thunder,
    It's such a blunder.

L ilapsophobia -
    Fearing tornadoes,
    However much I love potatoes,
    I will always, always hate tornadoes.

E isotrophobia -
    Fearing mirrors,
    One look in a mirror,
    Will make me shiver.

F ebriphobia -
> Fearing fevers,
> Colds, sweat, it's coming nearer,
> That nauseous feeling of a fever.

E cclesiophobia -
> Fearing church,
> If I lose my religion I have to search,
> In the creepy, scary church.

A rachnaphobia -
> Fearing spiders,
> I hate spiders,
> They're such good climbers.

R habadophobia -
> Fearing magic,
> Although it looks tragic,
> It's only magic.

S amhainophobia -
> Fearing Hallowe'en,
> I hate to scream,
> Especially on Hallowe'en.

Michael Larcombe (12)

Away With Words

I'm reading a book
A mysterious book
It's characters are so dark
With sentences so real
So real, I can feel their power to mark.

Words like:
Spooky, creepy, scary
Creaky, night, fright
Lonely, dark, pitch-black,
Which lead me to flight.

But they are only words, away with them.

Seren Jones (12)

Months

January, a frail, delicate, cold-hearted man,
Ragged and silent as the grave.
Half-starved, crouched on a blanket of white snow,
Dead eyes staring into space.

Until February arrived,
A cold face, hair constructed of icicles.
This young woman covered in snow,
An elegant figure in a long robe.

March dances into view, hair red as fire,
Windswept, wavy as the sea.
Her magnificent staff banished snow,
Snowdrops scattered everywhere to celebrate.

April had two faces,
Little, weak, mild were these delicate twins.
One of them discontented, dismal;
The other, cheerful, in embroidered rainbow belt.

Swept into space was beautiful Mother May.
A singing nightingale, birds resting in her thick hair.
Butterflies fanning her striking face,
Flower garlands everywhere.

A pretty child was gentle June.
Delicate face, sea-blue laughing eyes,
Fair complexion, bouquet full of roses,
Bluebirds perched on her shoulder.

July, a cheeky, mischievous fellow,
Like a goblin dressed in emerald leaves.
His impish face was wonderfully warm,
Sitting in front of the summer scarlet, sunset sky.

A purple-faced, beefy man was August,
His eyes full of rage.
He was yelling as fire descended from his mouth
And lightning struck at his side.

In the distance appeared September,
A motherly-like woman dressed in a woolly shawl.
Her woven basket full
Of mouth-watering fruit and nuts.

October proceeded behind September,
Windswept hair which held tattered leaves.
Ruby-red, lemon-yellow and fiery orange,
Against thick waves of auburn hair.

November was a pretty girl with her vivid shadow,
Sparkly hair, animals resting inside her thick coat.
A spider's lair was being spun in her hair
Which fell around her misty little face.

Finally December, a cheerful-faced youngster,
Ruby-red robins flew in her white freckled face.
Colourful decorations sparkled on her clothes
And a cross was drawn on her warm, caring heart.

Emily Lewis (13)

Sea Whisper

Wispy hair flapping in the wind,
He stands with his head resting on the bottom bar of the railings -
Looking out to sea.
The current shows a different colour to the rest of the sea,
Shallow waves licking the bottom of square-cut boulders,
Standing in line, between the breakwaters, like a row of soldiers.
A bitter wind blows off the evening sea and makes him squint a little.
With each small wave, the sea creeps further up
the small pebbly gaps between the boulders.
The smell of the sea blows past him along the coast,
And he stands silent and still,
Watching the seagulls as they transport him to another place.

Aimee Determann (12)

Life Of A Chair

First I started out at a lab,
Acid, rats and strange objects.
Got rid of me when I began to rust,
Then I ended up in a back garden.
At first I was nothing but a pigeon toilet,
But one day I was packed into a suitcase
And ended up in Las Vegas,
With a star role in an act.

I entered showbiz with seven more roles,
The make-up the anti-rust, it just isn't worth it.
Ended up as nothing, rusting in a skip,
Never to fulfil my dream.
It's kind of a shame, my mum was a seat at Old Trafford,
And my dad was a jet seat.
I'm a nobody, rusting away in a skip,
A rusting pile of waste.

My dream you say, that's simple,
To be used as a weapon, on Wrestlemania's Championship Match,
And to be held high in the air at the challenger's grasp
                                        and to be remembered.
But I'm a nothing, I'm a rusty bum,
Living on the streets in back alley skips.
I am ashamed, I was a waste from the start.

But as long as I live, which won't be long,
I'll always know how I tried to reach the top,
How I almost got there, but I was robbed.
It was true what dad said,
'Never go into showbiz, you'll end up as nothing.'

Dad was right, I will never achieve my goals,
I could have been a weapon at Madison Square Gardens,
I could have scored,
I could have contended.

Owen Jenkins (12)

The Sad Year

You sat in your chair,
Something happened to your hair,
It's all gone now,
But only you know how.

You stopped to read
And you stopped to plant seeds,
Of course you had cancer,
But how did people answer?

Your garden became messy,
And what about your aunt Bessy?
She cared for you
And your sister and brother too.

You started to get tired and go to bed,
You even started to put a hat on your head.
You couldn't walk,
You couldn't even talk.

They moved the bed downstairs,
Because you couldn't walk upstairs.
You laid there every day,
Nothing to pay.

You were asleep,
You'd have nothing to eat.
But one morning you couldn't breathe,
That was a good way to see you leave.

All your family were there
And by your bed there was an untouched pear.
Then the next Monday there it was,
The funeral.

It was a lovely way to say goodbye.
Everyone came,
All your friends who lived nearby,
Lots of speeches, lots of songs.

So they said goodbye to a
Husband, brother, dad, grandfather and a dear friend.

Bethan Hallett (12)

Doggy Lunar 10

There once was a dog who plodded along
making a tremendous noise.
He admired himself wildly,
through stamina, physique and poise.
But once he floated up to space
not to come back again.
I see that dog once a day,
his name's Doggy Lunar 10.

Shelby Rooney (11)

Away With Words

They took me galloping
On the shore
By the river
Through closed doors

They took me away
To new-found places
Places of beauty
Wonder and graces

Down by the lake
Where the sun shone bright
Into the forest
Where there was no light

Up to the clouds
Down to the core
They took me anywhere
And words take me more.

Hope Bolger
Austin Friars St Monica's School, Carlisle

Away With Words

Words make you smile,
Words are romantic,
Words may amaze you,
Words are fantastic.

Words can be so sweet,
Words can be kind,
Words may not mean anything,
Words may blow your mind.

Words are spoken out,
Every second of the day,
They can be good or bad,
But please say them in a sweet way.

Words can make you shiver,
Thinking of them day and night,
They may make you feel better,
And at last help you find the light.

Remember words create feelings,
So don't break someone's heart,
Careful how you use them,
They are an expressive form of art.

Christina Garbi (12)
Austin Friars St Monica's School, Carlisle

Away With Words

'Quack,' said the duck,
who was covered in slime,
'I need to wash this off,
in a very short time.'

'Oink,' said the pig,
who was eating some mush,
'I need a diet,
and something lush.'

'Moo,' said the cow,
who had stood on a nail,
'I'm clumsy and fat,
and could stand in a gale.'

'Blub,' said the sea lion,
who had eaten a fish,
' I need to learn to swim,
so I can stop eating this dish.'

'Argh,' said the animals
hearing each other speak,
'we must be hallucinating,
for there is a gas leak'.

Ben Hodgkiss (13)
Austin Friars St Monica's School, Carlisle

Away With Words

Down in the alley
Gone like the wind
Making his way
Or some kind of thing

Winding his way
Through store after store
So much he has
But he still wants more

Police arrive
With flashing blue lights
Surrounded he is
Oh what a sight

Hide the loot
Then comes surrender
Caught red-handed
Not much splendour

Questioned he is
But he's away with the birds
Not much to say
Lost for words.

Rosalind Sutcliffe (12)
Austin Friars St Monica's School, Carlisle

In The African Sun

Away on a plane to a foreign land,
With Africa surrounding, feeling lost and yet found,
Words and new meanings difficult to understand.

Great plains stretching for miles on end,
As vast as the oceans rolled into one,
Thousands of animals, on which to depend?
As detailed as a fingerprint etched with ink.

African deserts ancient and scarred, buzzing with life,
The ground crisp and baked in the scorching sun,
Animals that gallop, leap, race and chase from the old to the young,
Suddenly an indescribable noise, piercing silence, poacher, gun.

A short distance away the landscape changes dramatically,
From vast countryside, to the loud hustle and bustle of a city,
Rich, poor, needy, everyone has a category,
So many words all spoken at once, so confusing.

Words used in worship, soulful tribal songs and enchanting prayers,
Insults and criticism, damaging and pointless,
A word for everything, anything, nothing,
Words can be the most powerful things.

Away from din and pollution of the city, back on the African plains,
Where you can see for miles until the land collides with the sky,
Bursting into an ecstatic sunset of blurred red, yellows and oranges,
Slowly changing, a blanket of stars unfolding on black.

Away the day, now the moon and stars reappear,
With Africa shining, alight with fantasy, legend and truth,
Words can only describe how wonderful life really is!

Kate McNulty (13)
Austin Friars St Monica's School, Carlisle

What To Do

I've got a poem to write,
Thirty lines and no more.
What words to use?
What subject to choose?
Oh, here's an idea!

If I could change the world,
I would live in a chocolate house,
And eat a three-course chocolate meal.
Oh, that's no good!
My house would melt and I'd get fat!

If I could change the world,
I'd have a cleaner to clean my room,
And do my homework too.
Oh, that's no good!
The cleaner would get lost in the mess!

If I could change the world,
I'd own a jet,
And have a pilot called Jeeves.
Oh, that's no good!
I hate flying and Jeeves is a very uncommon name!

If I could change the world,
I'd have a yacht,
With a driver who'd teach me to drive.
Oh, that's no good!
Where would I sail it?

If I could change the world,
I wouldn't,
Because I'd never decide what to change.
The poem writing may not have gone well,
But I did write thirty lines.

Laura Wisdom (13)
Austin Friars St Monica's School, Carlisle

Groovin' Words

Words groovin'
Keep 'em moving
Get da beat going
Go wid da flow
Don't let 'em go

Shout 'em!
Scream 'em!
Show 'em wat you fink of 'em!
Don't matta wat u fink
Jus' giv it a go n u'll never no

Words dunnit mean anyfin
Needs no concentration
Jus a larl bit of imagination
To get da rhythm of da best

Words jumbling!
Words jumbling!
No mumbling!
No mumbling!

Jus scream 'em!
Scream 'em!
Jus scream 'em out loud!

Kate Scott (12)
Austin Friars St Monica's School, Carlisle

Away With Words

Words have great power
They can do magical things
They're the makers of good times or bad
They can make anything grow wings

It depends on the way you say them
What different words can mean
Shout 'em, whisper 'em, say 'em like you mean 'em
Tell the whole world where you've been

Words build relationships
Whether they are old or new
Make people love or hate you
Giving them their own view

Simple words can change your life
Love, or yes, or no
Will you just reject this question
Or will you decide to go?

You never know what's coming next with words
They are an endless wonder
Will you make the right decision
Or will you make a blunder?

Sarah Calvert (13)
Austin Friars St Monica's School, Carlisle

Away With Words

Words was a man,
A man with great pride.
He worked for the king
As his well paid scribe.

Once Words woke up
With a pain in his head,
He arrived in the throne room,
But the king was dead.

Words was caught
And framed for the crime.
He was charged with murder
And was jailed for a time.

Whilst in jail,
Words had a plan.
If he succeeded
He would be a free man.

On the roof of the prison
He built a plane.
He turned on the engine
And was free again.

So away with Words,
Up to the sky,
Where there's no pain and torture,
To the clouds he would fly.

Peter Relph (14)
Austin Friars St Monica's School, Carlisle

Cromber

Cromber is:
A man,
Who likes ham,
And cooks it in a pan.

He lurks in the shadows,
When he's eating marshmallows.
He comes out at night,
He likes to take a bite
At a child who is nice and fat.

He lurks like a cat.
He sleeps on a mat.

Cromber bites, kicks, hits and spits,
He can climb a wall,
And he's about four foot tall,
And likes playing ball.

He's as quick as a flash,
His nickname is Dash,
Beware, he throws mash,
And he likes to *smash.*

He is bad at school,
But he is really cool,
But sometimes acts like a fool.

Robert Dixon (11)
Austin Friars St Monica's School, Carlisle

Away With Words

Words paint pictures
Words sing songs
Words build relationships
Words can go wrong

Words open up the mind
Words form lies
Words take you far away
Words catch spies

Words create new life
Words destroy things
Words are exotic places
Words kill kings

Words are the beginning
Words are the end
Words make the world go round
Words are emotions you send

Words are the future
Words are the past
Words pass on wisdom
Once said, they last

Words are angry
Words are sad
Words are full of love and joy
Words wrongly picked are bad

Words are bright ideas
Words fulfil dreams
Words are the most precious gift
Words flow like streams.

Helena Wilson (12)
Austin Friars St Monica's School, Carlisle

Away With Words

I dunno what 2 write about,
I dunno what 2 do,
It's gonna take me ages,
And I can't just copy U.

There's 2 many things 2 think about,
2 many words 2 choose,
I don't stand a chance in dis class,
I know I'm gonna lose.

Twenty-six letters,
Millions of words,
I wish it could be simple,
Like tweet-tweet wiv the birds.

I've finally finished dis poem,
I don't know whether it's good,
I cud have got my parents 2 help,
But I don't know if they would.

Natasha Wannop (12)
Austin Friars St Monica's School, Carlisle

Away With Words

If music has a silver sound
As't rings around and round and round,
What place for words?

A picture's worth a thousand words,
And it can show the rarest bird,
What use are words?

A swan upon an inky pool
Is white, is black, its feet are cool -
Away with words!

Yet without words what shall we do?
How shall thoughts pass from me to you?
We need our words
For all we do.

Stuart Wheatcroft (16)
Austin Friars St Monica's School, Carlisle

The Poachers

I strolled on the savannah plain,
Seeing things I never wished to see.
When a great pride of lions padded off,
Not far away from me.
I saw what they'd been looking at,
And I'm very sad to say
A dead elephant lay on the floor,
With her tusks all hacked away.
I saw her baby pound across,
With panic in his eyes,
And try to nudge his mum to life
With little breathy sighs.
I could not tell him it's too late,
Your Mum's already gone,
But leaving him to panic
Would have seemed so very wrong.
I ran to find a ranger
Who could keep his future bright,
But when the ranger and I returned
We saw a sorry sight.
The mum and baby lay on the floor,
They lay so very still,
How could two poor animals die
When only one was killed?
Why don't they rip their own hair out?
Sell their own skin and bone?
The poachers kill these creatures,
But why can't they leave them alone?

Mairéad Merritt (12)
Castle Rushen High School, Castletown

Climate Change

Climate change,
Is simple but strange.
It is something we all need to fight!

If we fly on a plane,
We should be given the cane,
And sit in a room without light!

We are killing poor bear,
And giving humans a scare,
Or you could call it a fright!

Now that's just a bit,
So don't think that's it,
And just do as much as you can!

Inge Perry (11)
Castle Rushen High School, Castletown

The Bombings In Iraq

The bombings in Iraq
They never seem to stop
Citizens die and their soldiers don't
The bombings in Iraq

The bombings in Iraq
The British soldiers try to stop
Soldiers die in an attempt to stop
The bombings in Iraq

The bombings in Iraq
Gunshots and explosions
Day and night in an attempt to stop
The bombings in Iraq.

Robert Bell (11)
Castle Rushen High School, Castletown

Life Of A Very Small Baby

Grandma's eyes are never dry,
It's Daddy's sweet lu-a-by,
It's Mummy's gift and Grandma's blessing,
It's not protesting, it's life is small,
But over all it's happiness until it's gone.

It's a tear shed,
It's a cry for help that it'll never get,
When Mum appears and finds the small baby dead.
It's cold skin and very thin,
And very dim breathing, it stops and nothing.

Daddy's shouting,
Granddad's cursing and Grandma's screaming.
Mummy's not taking sides,
She cries,
The baby has said its final goodbyes.

Alex Cooke (12)
Castle Rushen High School, Castletown

Climate Change

C limate change has to change.
L ights need to be switched off to save energy.
I f we don't do something soon
M e and you will be in serious danger.
A gain and again we are told to change, but we don't.
T ogether we can change the future
E arth is in danger of destruction and it's our fault.

C limate change will happen unless we do something about it fast
H ands on and help the world
A rctic is melting too quickly
N either humans nor animals will live in a hundred years
G lobal warming is upon us
E nergy is going rapidly, so change!

Bethany Hall (11)
Castle Rushen High School, Castletown

Footballers' Behaviour

F ootballers' behaviour,
O ver-rated values,
O f the idolised players,
T o throw it back in the fan's faces
B ecause of bad behaviour,
A bad example to youngsters,
L ots of swearing.
L eisure for them is supposed to be football.
E xcept for a few who enjoy nightclubs more.
R epellant some because of referees' decisions,
S ome do the right thing.

B ehaviour says a lot about
E very single player.
H owever swearing and fighting can have
A serious effect for the player and his team,
V iolence is not the way to act,
I gnoring the rules,
O ur youth idolise these players.
U tmost players even do it.
R igid are the youngsters' minds who see these incidents.

Mason McLarney (11)
Castle Rushen High School, Castletown

Extinct

The human population is quickly growing
While endangered species are rapidly going
Their habitats are shrinking in size
But no one seems to realise

Animals are dying because of pointless needs
Catching the car instead of working your knees
Such innocent creatures are getting wiped out
And now I've realised, it's time to stand up and shout:
Save the animals, help the trees
Stop pollution, prevent disease!

Liam Dixon (11)
Castle Rushen High School, Castletown

Families

L ove is precious
O h, tender care
V aries with families everywhere
E veryone has someone who loves them

P eople want to make peace
E veryone should help
A ngry, cross terrorists
C rying people
E veryone wants to make peace

C are is priceless
A mazing as life can be
R are it may be
E veryone cares for someone

F amily is a great thing
A lmost everyone loves theirs
M y family, I love mine a lot
I 've fought and lied
L ove your family
Y ou'll do fine.

Chelsie Harrison (12)
Castle Rushen High School, Castletown

Leave Our Trees Alone

Every day, every second, trees are cut down.
They're killing the animals as they fall to the ground.

It's happening in Africa, South America too.
Why do people think there is nothing we can do?

We can stop all this by not using wood.
If we carry on like this the Earth will just go to mud.

The forests and trees are the lungs of the lands,
This Earth's fate is in our hands.

Josh Gardner (11)
Castle Rushen High School, Castletown

Extinct

Dolphins swim through the sea
Somersaulting and jumping through the air
Soon they will all be gone

Tigers whizz through forests
But soon no loud roar will be heard
For soon they will all be gone

Polar bears crash through the ice
Drenching their coat of white fur
Soon they will all be gone

Elephants wash their giant bodies
Playfully splashing about
Soon they will all be gone

Slowly all these animals will be extinct
They are all dying
Soon they will be all gone.

Lucy Richardson (11)
Castle Rushen High School, Castletown

Battery Farms

Your meat that you eat is treated badly
twenty-four million chickens
are cooped in pygmy cages
and lights shining on them 24/7
'cause supermarkets can't be patient
so animals are battery fed
to make them grow faster and faster
let's protest this cruelty and madness
and save all the poor farm animals
get them out of the teeny cages
set them free in open spaces
so they have a good life.

Elizabeth Power (12)
Castle Rushen High School, Castletown

The Earth Is Dying

With mass deforestation,
Just to support our population,
The ozone is opening,
It will be the end of our nation.

The polar caps are melting,
The core of the Earth will cool,
And all of this will be happening,
While I'm writing this in school.

The summers will get warmer,
The winters shall make us freeze,
And don't forget that we have to stop
The rising of the seas.

Most of this has been on the news,
So now is the time to choose,
Should we go back to the older ways,
Or never see the rest of our days?

Thomas Chard (12)
Castle Rushen High School, Castletown

The Rising Flood

The sea whizzing through the Earth,
Wind whistling through the trees,
Waves crash and break the rocks.

Rain crashes down below,
Clouds fill with rain and hail.
Wind flows through the leaves and the trees are left bare.

The waves yawn and swallow rocks, trees,
Hundreds of ships, houses and farms.

Animals run for safety as the flood breaks,
Birds fly high,
Fish swim for deep water as the flood rises,
People scream and run as the rustling flood rises.

Megan McCarter (11)
Castle Rushen High School, Castletown

Young Writers - Away With Words Around The UK

Climate Change

Climate change is big in the news,
We don't have a chance to choose.

It it will happen to us all
Then the human race will fall.

Icebergs meting into the sea,
Polar bears have no chance to flee.

In ten year's time you will able to see
What is happening to you and me.

Polluted air over our head,
In millions of year's time we will all be dead.

In this last verse I hope to say,
In millions of years we will be OK.

Matthew Gardner (11)
Castle Rushen High School, Castletown

Global Warming

Global warming is hard to explain,
It kills everything in its way.

Mother Earth is dying,
And soon will be left crying.

We need to stop it now,
So that the temperature goes down.

Burning hot temperature was not here in the past,
But we are still the last to know.

We have to stop it before it gets out of hand,
Just stop and think about Nature's land.

Jenny Turner (11)
Castle Rushen High School, Castletown

What's In Your Lunch Box

What's in your lunch box?
What do you eat?
Five portions of fruit and veg,
And lots of red meat?

Apples, grapes,
That's the stuff you adore,
Or maybe some celery,
And carrots galore!

Or maybe you're unhealthy,
You crave for something sweet,
Caramels, chocolate bars,
That's the stuff you like to eat!

It's OK to have some chips,
But not all the time.
So take my advice,
Listen to this rhyme.

You should be healthy,
Active and fit,
But it's OK to have some chocolate,
As long as it's just a bit.

Heather Allen (11)
Castle Rushen High School, Castletown

Crime Poem

Guns should be left
Stop car crime and theft
Raids should be stopped
And weapons dropped

Knives should be discarded
Yobs should be red-carded
They should stop them getting beer and drugs
To stop them getting in gangs with thugs.

Richard Radcliffe (11)
Castle Rushen High School, Castletown

Speed

S peed is a dangerous thing.
P olice urgent to stop the madness.
E xtreme speeding is what they like.
E nergy pumping around the body,
D eath lingers all around!

K illing lots in fatal crashes,
I nvestigators trying to figure it out,
L ights come down on the site,
L oving memories for those that died.
S peed kills! Don't you forget that!

The first letter of every line,
Spells out an important message.
Now let's stop the speed and save lives.

James Harrison (11)
Castle Rushen High School, Castletown

Deforestation

D eath to animals,
E aters of leaves suffer.
F orest fires kill many,
O pen land made for farmers.
R evolutions are caused,
E xtinction occurs.
S uffocating gases rise into the air,
T rees are special, so don't destroy.
A nimals lose homes,
T errible losses throughout countries.
I neffectual people try to stop this.
O utcry us, all who care,
N ow please do something, not just for our welfare!

Breeshey Mort (12)
Castle Rushen High School, Castletown

Animal Extinction

I only want to make the place a better one,
One that's exciting, beautiful and fun.
Just think if you've left your TV on standby,
You have kissed a panda's life goodbye.
And if you've left your car running too long
No one will hear another macaw's song.
I only want to make this place a better one,
One that's exciting, beautiful and fun.

I only want to make this place a better one,
One that's exciting, beautiful and fun.
Just think if everyone has left their lights on,
The whole race of the chimpanzee will be gone.
We are already decreasing their numbers,
But please don't send them into their slumbers.
I only want to make this place a better one,
One that's exciting, beautiful and fun.

I only want to make this place a better one,
One that's exciting, beautiful and fun.
Oh why did we have to do this?
This world was simply bliss,
The ice is melting far too fast,
So fast the polar bears will be in the past.
I only want to make this place a better one,
One that's exciting, beautiful and fun.

Alex Maitland (11)
Castle Rushen High School, Castletown

Animal Extinction

Poor little animals roaming the Earth,
So different from what it was like at their birth.

Ever heard the expression, *as dead as a dodo?*
It came from killing, an almighty no-no!

The extinction list, growing bigger every day,
It shouldn't be, that's what some people say.

Lonely animals, dropping dead one by one,
Before long they will all be gone!

Being killed for their skins, tusks and bones,
But no one thinks of animals all alone.

Extinct!

Jade Booth (11)
Castle Rushen High School, Castletown

Football Frenzy

Players walk onto the pitch, as thousands of fans cheer them on,
the match begins, the stadium erupts,
with noises of horns, drums and song,
as one foul turns into more,
it turns into a war,
as two players start barging,
the goalkeeper's charging,
as a fury of fists pounds down hard,
the security comes in,
someone's broken their shin.
If two players had kept their cool
the children wouldn't fight at school.

Fraser Veale (11)
Castle Rushen High School, Castletown

Animal Extinction

A nimal extinction is becoming worse
N ot a single animal can escape it
I dle humans don't think about it
M ammals are eaten and skinned
A mphibians are eaten and killed for sport
L emurs have no trees to live in

E nvironment is being threatened
X mas without a turkey, goose or chicken
T rees are cut down, with buildings in their place
I nfant animals also cannot escape it
N early all animals might be gone
C learly something must be done
T rees are our source of oxygen, as well as animals
I ndescribable amounts of trees are chopped down
O rdeals over war are making it forgotten
N ever has it been this bad.

Kelly Firth (12)
Castle Rushen High School, Castletown

Animal Extinction

Soon we won't have animals at all,
All their fur will be on coats at the mall.

Moles, birds, fish and hares,
Even soon, no polar bears.

Soon every animal will be dead,
Maybe some of them a hat on our head.

Many dolphins are killed each year,
Don't let the others be in fear.

Everyone can make a change,
Think of all the animals we can save.

Ellie Harrison (12)
Castle Rushen High School, Castletown

What Is War?

What is war?
That game they play.
That game of selfishness and greed.
Who can take the most people's lives?
Where the bellowing guns drown out the sound of screaming men.
When you may not ever see your wife again.
Sounds like fun doesn't it?

They invited me to come along.
But I didn't want to play . . .
What a shame they made me.
'Goodbye,' I said, 'I might not be back for dinner.'
Not for the next couple of years or so.
Hundreds of us men, marching side by side.
Not daring to step a foot out of line.
I look around at my team . . . I might not see you tomorrow.

A few days later
Wow! I'm still in the game . . .
They haven't killed me yet.

Lisa Sabine (14)
Chace Community School, Enfield

Fields Of Sorrow

I wade across the fields of sorrow,
hoping war will end tomorrow.
So many deaths, no one can win,
as many die as days have been.
Solemn soldiers shooting shells,
why was I put in this hell?
So many friends lie by me dead,
the sounds of war swirl in my head.
I wade across the fields of sorrow,
is there no chance of peace tomorrow?

Emily Hart (14)
Chace Community School, Enfield

Perfection

Winter becomes spring,
The darkness fades away,
When you bless me with,
With yourself divine.

Oh you,
You so perfect,
You so peerless,
Created by the gods,
I'll be yours,
Let me be yours.

My heart to your service,
Your loyal slave,
Your most loyal servant,
I'll lie for you,
I'll cry for you,
I'll kill for you,
I'll die for you.

Nicola Lewis (14)
Chace Community School, Enfield

Autumn

Leaves on the trees
Leaves on the street
Leaves everywhere
I wonder if there are
Still leaves on the trees.
It is cold outside
Because it is autumn
And it is very windy.
Rain falls on my head
As I lead the way.

Miten Hirani (11)
Copland Community School, Wembley

Life Is A Puzzle

My life is full of questions
I don't know where to start
Bit of pieces everywhere
Just waiting to make a whole again.

Who, what, when and why
What do I intend to find this time?
I am incomplete
So many pieces of me are missing.

There's an eager person inside me
Wanting to find out the truth
Confusion
Should I or not?

I have had enough
I must complete the puzzle
The puzzle that has been jumbled
For the whole of my life.

Amura Abdullahi (14)
Copland Community School, Wembley

The Day And Night

The stars are bright,
They give us their light,
In day they're out of sight,
They only show at night.

The moon is white,
Sometimes gives us a fright,
They always write,
A story of fight.

The sun is hot,
It can melt a pot,
It can burn a boat
And a goat.

Hardik Rohitkumar (12)
Copland Community School, Wembley

Two Different Worlds

S amira is my name
T en is my age
O ngoing battles are all that surround me
P alestine is my home

W ar has destroyed it and only left a shadow of what it once was
A ll I have left is me and the tattered clothes on my body
R est in peace is all I have left to say

U nderground is where my family lay
N o more hope as all that's left is pain and death
I feel numb like the merciless bombs that fall from the sky . . .
T ina is my name
E ight is my age

I have my mummy and daddy and a big house too
N ice clothes fill my wardrobe

L ondon is my home, a city full of fun
O rlando is our next holiday destination!
V aluable jewellery adorns my neck
E ndless choices to make about my life - because I have rights.

Azzah ElHabashy (14)
Copland Community School, Wembley

The Sea

The sea is beautiful you see,
Nobody knows when it will stop,
Everyone plays on the beach,
Especially everyone eats peach on that particular day.

The sea is sometimes warm.
Also the summer makes the sunshine warm in the sea.
The sea and the sun brings out the love and happiness in everyone

The sea is magical and wonderful,
As well the waves are magical too.
The sea is magical as always.

Amina Marzouki (14)
Copland Community School, Wembley

My Relationship With A Piano

I play the piano, it's my pleasure,
I wish I could play it forever and ever.
It's my inspiration,
Even on vacation.
Why do I love it so?
I guess I will never know.
Strange, I love a piano and no other instrument,
As important as a stamen and a filament.
You could play a happy or sad song,
A song short or long.
Or is it the elegance that captures me most?
The keys as smooth as a knife in butter.
Every key from one to another,
I feel as at home as with my mother.

Zennah Mogul (13)
Copland Community School, Wembley

I Love Football

I've got soccer magazines and soccer books
And scarves and boots and kits on hooks.
I think about it when I'm drinking tea
And while I'm sitting watching TV.
I think about it elsewhere too
Like in the kitchen and in the loo.
I think about it in the bath
And while I'm walking down the garden path.
I think about it everywhere
Like when I'm washing my short black hair.
I think about it in boring school
And when I go swimming at the pool.
So this is how I love my football
So don't try to beat me 'cause you will fail.

Walid Aimaq (12)
Copland Community School, Wembley

The Darkness

As the darkness in me is slowly igniting
My willpower begins to burn bright
For my dreams begin fighting
While my soul yearns for the light
The darkness holds me and grabs my desires
And begins to weaken my heart
It leads my fears higher and higher
And pulls my pride apart
I can feel it consuming me
Engulfing and feeding
Holding on so tightly
Seeking and heeding
I can feel it hurting me, screaming and staring
Slowly, watching, waiting
Appearing and disappearing
Getting envious, it begins hating
And slowly pulls my heart in the dark
As it searches me in and out
It leaves an invisible mark
It screeches loud and makes me shout
A piercing crash wakes me
It brings me back to reality
Although the thought was bearable
That it was all just a dream
The truth is more unbearable
Than how you want everything to seem.

Payal Patel (14)
Copland Community School, Wembley

War

Every time I look outside,
I hear the sorrow of the world.
It looks as if life itself has died,
It feels like I'm in the afterworld.
It seems like the world is lost to me,
I think I must disagree.

The leaves have fallen from the trees,
Houses broken into threes,
Someone has to stop my screams,
All my mum does is sneeze,
People fighting for no reason,
Lives are gone in threesomes,
I thought this war would end this season.

I thought we called ourselves civilised,
We go on taking human lives,
Every mother, every father, every daughter, every son,
All might survive except one,
Fire, bomb, plane and ship,
If you were here what would you think?

The sky is misty and grey,
The tension and atmosphere is scaring me away,
I run around looking for a corner to hide, like a stray,
I feel alone with no one to talk to all day.

Life is precious,
Cherish the life you have.

Amal Abdi (14)
Copland Community School, Wembley

Autumn

It's a cold, windy evening.
When all the children are sleeping at night,
The autumn leaves brushed away,
By the autumn light,
But now that winter has arrived,
Coldness is in the air and we survive.
When we wake up in the day,
Chill is coming in the air,
Everywhere we see snow,
Brushing by our window.
Lying in our cosy beds,
While Mum looks through the sheds.
We lie in bed,
While snow slips and slides outside.

Oltiana Dervishi (11)
Copland Community School, Wembley

Lightning Bolt

Lightning bolt, it's not my fault,
I'm playing with toys,
Trying to take my mind off this ear-piercing noise,
Today is a crazy day,
And I'm trying to get through this in every way,
I turn the music up loud,
And my dad says if I get through this he'll be proud,
Running and hiding,
Ducking and diving,
Trying my hardest to hide
From the noise that is hurting me so much inside.
I'm tired and I need to sleep,
In my bed I start to weep,
Lightning bolt, it's not my fault.

Rory Eduh (12)
Copland Community School, Wembley

The Routine

Every day is like the same day,
And we call this thing a routine,
You wake up and get dressed,
Then you have breakfast,
Put your shoes on, then
Kiss your family goodbye,
Instead of goodnight,
And also Dad took a flight
To see his mum in Morocco.
So here we are, I go to school to learn,
I found a worm in my lunch.
I came back home to eat my tea,
I went back to sleep.
The same thing tomorrow,
But my dad will be back from Morocco.

Hanaa Ennast Eldrissi (11)
Copland Community School, Wembley

Autumn

The autumn wind blows,
A nice warm duvet for when you're cold,
The lovely trees blow side to side,
Kids stay home to keep warm and hide.
The leaves falling nice and slow,
While winds swiftly pass and blow.
No one out to play,
Until the time comes for May.
Roads are quiet, no one around,
Empty stations underground,
Televisions on so loud,
Rain falls from the clouds.
Until the time that sun appears,
No more children to play and cheer.

Nasrina Hassan (12)
Copland Community School, Wembley

Cricket

I was an opener
I walked to the crease
My arms were shaking
Like jelly, I needed peace

The bowler marked his line
Ran into the crease
I got ready
I went down the ground and hit the ball for six

Their run rate went low
Ours was high
The next ball I hit
Went into the sky

Twenty balls later
My innings ended
I walked to the pavilion
I gave a clap and showed a shot, *defended!*

Ashish Patel (12)
Copland Community School, Wembley

Rich Man, Poor Man

Rich man, poor man,
They're worlds apart,
Only you can understand,
Looking forward, say a prayer,
For the next two thousand years.

We are one family across the world,
Different in so many ways,
We all need each other, so put your hand in mine,
Let's try to step together in time.

Fayola Mawulawde (11)
Copland Community School, Wembley

The Essence Of Time

I have been known,
To be of the essence.
I cannot be shown,
Yet you fear my presence.

Past, present, future,
Can be my name.
It is in my nature,
To drag you into my game.

When you need me most,
I flee fast.
Like a ghost,
I'm renowned to fly past.

I lead you to fate and slip through your fingers,
For time never stops, nor lingers.

Shalin Patel (14)
Copland Community School, Wembley

Global Warming

G reenhouse gases
L ow-lying areas flood
O zone layer is getting thinner
B urning fossil fuels every day
A nimals will become extinct
L and will be lost forever

W arming of the Earth
A ircraft relasing carbon dioxide
R aise in global temperature
M elting of ice caps
I ncrease in rainfall in tropical areas
N itrogen oxides and hydrocarbons from exhaust fumes
G reenhouse effect
    Are all effects or causes of *global warming!*

Luke James Phillips (14)
Dyffryn School, Port Talbot

Never Forget . . .

(Dedicated to Hannah Lawrence)

Never forget: they travelled hundreds of miles
To face their trials
Now we pay tribute
For what they did contribute.

Never forget: their journey was long and hard
But it was no façade
Now they lie; unknown
In fields yet to be sown.

Never forget: they went too young
But on the road still they sung
They fought in Hell
But were left where they fell.

Never forget: battles took place on land, sea and air
But they didn't seem to care
They fought with fearless guile
In the trenches mile on mile.

Never forget: in the trenches rats scurry
As men go down in the slurry
Officers die with honour
But the T*ommie* is a goner.

Never forget: as ammo runs low
Home; men want to go
As men climb the ladders
With worry, full are their bladders.

Never forget: deserters are shot without honour or glory
But the battles are much more gory
Gallons of blood are spilt
Mixed with disease, bacteria and silt.

We will never forget those who fought and died for country
But the spoils of war are only monetary.

Robert Oxley (16)
Enfield Grammar School, Enfield

WWE Entertainer

In the locker room, poised, ready to go,
Sweat running down my neck,
Nerves getting the better of me.
It is time to entertain.

The long walk of fear to reach my peak,
Deserted, just me, myself and I,
The hullabaloo, the uproar of the crowd.
It is time to entertain.

Heart pounding, pulsating, racing,
Goosebumps all over,
Hair's standing up tall and firm.
It is time to entertain.

Phenomenally nerves starting to die down,
Courage overruling, I am at my peak,
But a moment away,
It is time to entertain.

Electrifying, exhilarating, stimulating,
Walking down the platform,
Crowd cheering my name,
It is time to entertain.

Kunal Patel (13)
Enfield Grammar School, Enfield

The Lonely Boy

Alone and scared sits the lonely boy
Not cared for, not loved
All he has, a ripped cuddly toy
Alone and scared sits the lonely boy

He walks down the street
Bad thoughts on his mind
Others don't know
They might as well be blind
Alone and scared sits the lonely boy

When the boy gets home
Dad raises his fists
Preparing his strikes
And hits the boy, as hard as he likes
Alone and scared sits the lonely boy

His mum can't take it
She just can't cope
She's having sex with another bloke
Alone and scared sits the lonely boy

Dad's getting angry
Time is running out
He rants and raves and gives the boy a clout
Alone and scared sits the lonely boy.

Ben Twitchings (14)
Enfield Grammar School, Enfield

More Than Friends

A single smile turns my heart around
A single tear could make the sun fall down

I wouldn't call us just friends
I wouldn't call her my lover instead

Lovers come and go
Knowing she'll always be around me makes me feel at home

Mountains I would move for her
If she got ill I would find the cure

She calls me her hero
Without her I would be zero

Do I love her? I ask myself
If I ever feel love it's because of her

We're more than just friends
But less than lovers.

Samuel Ampah (16)
Enfield Grammar School, Enfield

The Bomb Scare

In 1941
How the school was run
Every day there was a bomb scare
London was in despair
Our mothers were wearing skirts
Our fathers were in Dunkirk
German planes were bombing
The girls were sobbing
Under the desks they pray
For the bombs to go astray
But here it was safe to stay
Because in Germany we lay.

Max Schultz (12)
Enfield Grammar School, Enfield

Black

No sight to see,
The world is black,
Sight is the key,
And that is what I lack.

The world is nothing,
Emptiness, colourless,
As I see nothing,
I am harmless.

Life is blank,
I can hear, I can speak,
It feels like a prank,
My senses have a leak.

I cannot see anything,
I just imagine it all,
The whole world, everything,
I feel like a fool.

I am blind,
I cannot see,
No sight to find,
He, she or me.

Ajay Mehta (12)
Enfield Grammar School, Enfield

Sunshine Is A Wonderful Thing

Sunshine is a wonderful thing.
It puts a smile on my face.
It's like a big, cheesy grin,
But way, way up in space.

It never makes me frown,
The sun I never hate,
Until the sun goes down,
When it gets late.

Aimee Renouf (12)
Grainville School, Jersey

My Holiday Fun

Friday I am going away
In Dubai for a week I will stay
My mum and dad, Abby and me
To a hotel, right by the sea!

Swimming, shopping, skiing and more
That spells fun, excitement galore
We're all together having fun
Chatting, playing in the hot sun!

Charlotte Luce (12)
Grainville School, Jersey

The Big Mistake

We came back from our honeymoon
All was in care
Our visitor was coming soon
It could only be Claire

Soon she arrived
With a quick knock at the door
I could see something strange in her eyes
I just wasn't quite sure
I looked from Claire to Paul
Then Paul to Claire
I thought my relationship is going to fall
Or is this an affair?

I went out of the room
But I had to spy
She kissed him like a baboon
I started to cry
I ran as fast as a dart
I shouted, 'What's going on here?'
I said to Paul, 'We have to part
Or have to move on, my dear.'

Libby Manifold (13)
Howell's School, Denbigh

Growing Up

What's happening to me, it's feeling rather strange
I was just a little girl and things began to change
Posters of horses and cats neatly pinned on my wall
Have been slowly replaced by Robbie, McFly
And some good-looking man with his football
I used to always be smiling and just plain happy
Now I can't help being moody and snappy!
Cartoons are out and music is in
Make-up is cool and you just have to be thin
Text messages from boys are much better than toys
Oh, little sister, you can be so in the way
Can't you find someone your own age to come and play?
Getting up in the morning is now not done with ease
And it's straight to the mirror, I have spots to squeeze!
All of this is really quite scary and a bit of a nightmare
Nobody said it would be like this, it's so unfair!

Anna Harrison (13)
Howell's School, Denbigh

Down Behind The Dustbin

(Based on 'Down Behind the Dustbin' by Michael Rosen)

Down behind the dustbin I met a dog called Molly,
and I said, 'What are you doing?'
and she said, 'Playing with my dolly.'

Down behind the dustbin I met a dog called Tate,
and I said, 'What are you doing?'
and he said, 'Playing with my mate.'

Down behind the dustbin I met a dog called Lee,
and I said, 'What are you doing?'
and he said, 'Playing with my key.'

Down behind the dustbin I met a dog called Flop,
and I said, 'What are you doing?'
and he said, 'Playing with my pot.'

Adrianne Tyson (13)
Howell's School, Denbigh

My Friends

My friends are brilliant,
I'm happy when they're around,
They're there when I need them most,
They make me smile when I'm down.

We always have fun together,
We always have ups and downs,
We always stick together,
Through the good times and bad.

My friends are special to me,
I treasure them greatly,
I'll keep them close to my heart,
Forever and always.

Olivia Waltho (12)
Howell's School, Denbigh

Slavery

My feet are dirty and sore
as I drag my bundle of rags
across the dusty floor.

Sun creeps through cracks in the wall
as I wait, wait to be sold -
then I hear a loud call.

Like cattle loaded on a van
not knowing where we're going or why,
we're now owned by this man.

My freedom I will miss
I'd like to decide for myself
I didn't want it like this.

Samantha Manolescue (13)
King Henry VIII School, Abergavenny

There's A Witch In My Class

There's a witch in my class
You wait and see
There's a witch in my class
And she'll get me

There's a witch in my class
She's as ugly as hell
There's a witch in my class
There goes the bell

There's a witch in my class
And I'm going home
There's a witch in my class
And I'm all alone

There's a witch in my class
And she's looking for me
There's a witch in my class
But I'm hiding you see

There's a witch in my class
I'm running very fast
There's a witch in my class
I'm nearly home at last

There's a witch in my class
I got home safely
There's a witch in my class
She can't come in, luckily

She thinks I'm small
She thinks I'm weak
She thinks I'm a coward
She thinks I'm a freak

So I think I'll stay at home
Where she can't get me
While I'm all alone
So she must let me be.

Emily Roberts (13)
King Henry VIII School, Abergavenny

Away With Words

I've been home all day,
On my own.
But that's how I like it,
It's so much better than when they come home.
  Shouting,
    Screaming,
      Swearing.

And then they turn on me.
He doesn't hit Mum,
He hits me.
I don't know why,
I don't even know what I've done wrong.
But even now, on my own,
I'm scared
I can only wait,
  w
  a
  i
  t
      Wait

What if he kills me this time?
He said he would.
Who would care?
Who would know?

Rachel Atkinson (13)
King Henry VIII School, Abergavenny

Away With Words

The knife came at me like a fish through water,
As it came closer my scream became louder,
I tried to run but my legs would not move,
The knife was coming and there was nothing I could do.

Christopher Brown (12)
King Henry VIII School, Abergavenny

Abuse Alphabet

A is for assault
B is for bullying
C is for cut
D is for death
E is for execution
F is for fist
G is for grievous
H is for hatred
I is for insult
J is for jagged
K is for kick
L is for life
M is for murder
N is for nobody
O is for orders
P is for punch
Q is for quarrel
R is for rebel
S is for sexual
T is for torture
U is for underestimate
V is for vulture
W is for wasted
X is xterminated
Y is for you
Z is for zap!

Henri Dobbs (12)
King Henry VIII School, Abergavenny

Summer

Ice-cold ice creams,
Burning orange sun.
Everlasting fun,
Late-night parties.
Clear yellow beaches,
Panting dogs.
Bees, butterflies, wasps.
Walks in the countryside,
Children playing in the street.
Boiling hot weather,
Swimsuits and flip-flops.
Games of football in the park,
Time out with our friends.
Camping in our sleeping bags,
In the moonlit brightness.
Saving electricity, always out,
Staying up for the sunset.
Missing the sunrise,
Back to school is the time I dread.
New school year, new teachers.
No time for playing now,
The sun's disappearing, winter's coming.
Can't wait for next year, the summer again.
Counting down the days to see what next summer brings!

Sam Morgan (14)
King Henry VIII School, Abergavenny

The Meaning Of Life

No one knows the real meaning of life
To me it's like a never-ending roller-coaster ride
That crashes to a halt when happiness is around
Butterflies floating past me with a glistening sound
My heart beats firmly
No one can stop this fabulous moment I've found
Smiling, laughing and screaming with joy
As life is appearing before my sparkling eyes
Until . . . all of a sudden sadness appears
My heart beats faster
Than a cheetah catching his prey
My tears come down as if they are
An ocean here to stay
Full of silence, darkness and loneliness
. . . Welcome to the real world

I think life is about what you do and what decisions you make
That might change your future and your feelings.

Rachel Byrne (13)
King Henry VIII School, Abergavenny

Bullying

Bullying is a terrible thing
When you bully you will never win
Think about the person on the receiving end
You are driving them round the bend.

They won't tell their parents
They will never know
How much they feel hurt
Believe me bullying doesn't work.

You will worry when someone finds out
Then you will start to pout
So think about what you have done, again
Would you like to be driven round the bend?

Catherine Pugh (11)
King Henry VIII School, Abergavenny

My Hero Tanni Grey-Thompson

Onward she went, fighting onward, upward, fly
Pushing limits to reach the top, the apex, the sky.

No legs could run but she could race,
A task that's hard, she did face,
But no excuse passed her mouth,
For she did work from top north and down to south.

Onward she did go, fighting onward, upward, fly
Pushing limits to reach the top, the apex, the sky.

Ambition pulsing through her every vein,
Even if she were in pain.
Wheels spinning, pushing on.
Passing her rivals, till she was gone,
Over that triumphant line,
The British flag worn as a sign,
Around her shoulder it would claim,
For my country I have gained.

Onward she went, fighting onward, up to the sky
Pushing limits to reach the top, the apex, to fly.

A simple chair that's all it be,
With strong, fast wheels that we can see,
But it was that fast and simple chair
That took her the long way there.
Along the track and to glory,
A living legend, a wonderful story.
For onward Tanni went, fighting onward, high
And reach, she did, the apex, the top, the sky.
A champion of one, we be proud,
For she is Welsh and of our crowd.

Katherine Taylor (13)
King Henry VIII School, Abergavenny

Good Times, Great Memories

I remember one time when I went to Oakwood,
I saw the Bounce and wanted to go on it,
And as I got closer I felt the ground shake,
Like I was caught in an earthquake,
It was only my legs trembling though,
Finally it was my turn,
And I went
U
U
P
P
Then suddenly
D
D
O
O
W
W
N
N
My stomach was rumbling,
And started a-tumbling,
And then back
U
P

D
O
W
N
And then slowly
U
U
P
P
P

I could see all the rides and hear loads of tiny voices
And then
D
D
O
O
W
W
N
N
Then I finally got off and *whoosh,*
I felt like I was floating on air.

Joe Hayward (12)
King Henry VIII School, Abergavenny

Déjà Vu

I have It in the day,
I have it in the night,
Sometimes at lunchtime

What is it?
I dream what is tomorrow,
It feels like a dream,
Why should I believe it?

What is it?

I still see it now,
I understand too,
I hope you do too.

It's déjà vu!

Ian Weed (11)
King Henry VIII School, Abergavenny

A Man Who Cannot See

A blind man who cannot see
How does he know that a bird's in a tree?
He hears it sing that's how he knows
Tweet, tweet, tweet, the birdie goes.

A blind man who cannot see
Feels the warm fire at his knee,
He knows it's there
Because of the smell in the air
And he can hear the snap and crackle.

A blind man who cannot see
Knows what the weather will be,
He can feel the wind in his hair
So he knows the sun's not there.

Robert Fitzpatrick (12)
King Henry VIII School, Abergavenny

Turning Time

If time could turn itself back,
stop the great ship hitting the ice,
sending souls beyond the stars
and bodies to the gloomy depths.

If time could turn itself back,
stop the tyrant's disease spreading across the world,
leaving the innocent to suffer
at the hands of a dictator.

If time could turn itself back,
stop the tsunami of two thousand and four,
evacuate the area . . .
and save the lives of many more.

Kirsty Jones (13)
King Henry VIII School, Abergavenny

The Curse Of The Darkest Sin

It's closer that you've ever known
And its power's grown and grown
It has the power to destroy
It's the curse of the darkest sin!

And as it starts to take command
The veins turn black upon your hand
Dark wings emerge from your back
It's the curse of the darkest sin!

You can't begin to understand
The power held within your hand
This evil consumes from within
It's the curse of the darkest sin!

You can't control this great might
So search for shelter through the night
Because the sun will start to sting
It's the curse of the darkest sin!

To be rid of this great evil
You must find the dark lord's tower
Free him from his eternal
It's the curse of the darkest sin!

There is a price to pay for this
The lord shall open the abyss
And all things dark shall be released
It's the curse of the darkest sin!

Then you shall share your curse with all
Release him and the Earth will fall
But is freedom worth all of this?
It's the curse of the darkest sin!

You can't escape the darkest sin!
It haunts you and your next of kin!

Thomas Shankland (14)
King Henry VIII School, Abergavenny

Snow Day

As that first snowflake falls,
On a fresh, new winter's morn.
That one child that's still up,
Knows what's coming shortly in time,
So he sleeps and dreams of what will be.

Awoken from his quiet, undisturbed slumber,
He races downstairs, towards the radio,
To find what the day brings.
He waits for the few words he's longed for,
'The following schools are closed . . .'

He jumps with glee,
When his school is announced.
Fast as he can he gobbles his food,
His toast, bacon, eggs and juice,
He packs away his dishes and runs to his room.

He bursts through the door,
Blasts through the snow.
Sliding on the ice,
He flies down the road,
To grab a friend, so not to be alone.

They grab their sleds,
Glide further down,
Down to the nearest,
Steepest and snowiest hill
From all around.

Snowballs zooming,
Zooming from there, near and far.
Final snowflakes falling,
From the white sky above.
But all this ends with the pit-pat of rain!

Rory Havard (14)
King Henry VIII School, Abergavenny

Emotional Roller-Coaster

I cried when I fainted in class,
I cried because I felt weak,
I cried, angry at myself for feeling like that,
I'm not going to cry anymore.

This is not going to defeat me,
I will overcome these feelings,
I know I will regain control,
I know I am not weak, I'm simply human.

I cried, my friend hurt me,
I cried when she laughed and told me I was wrong,
I cried because I had let her hurt me,
I'm not going to cry anymore.

This isn't going to defeat me,
I will overcome these feelings,
I will prove the whole world wrong,
I can do it, and I'll do it on my own.

I cried because I felt alone.
I cried when no one was there.
I cried but I knew someone could help me,
I'm not going to cry anymore.

This isn't going to defeat me,
I will overcome these feelings,
I know I have it within me
To fight these feelings and win.

Sophie Rigby (14)
King Henry VIII School, Abergavenny

Jump

Jump,
Touch the sky, a new start.
Jump,
Release yourself from life's sticky tart.
Jump,
Fly like a new white dove.
Jump,
Take airs, newborn love.
Jump,
Follow life's long track.
Jump,
Go forward, don't look back.
Jump,
Go now, don't keep waiting.
Jump,
Leave behind anything worth hating.
Jump,
Just
Jump!

Justin Lines (11)
King Henry VIII School, Abergavenny

Moving On

I remember when I was young,
I used to have so much fun.

Screaming, shouting, running around,
Playing hide-and-seek under the ground.
My worries small until I grew tall.

My worries now, overall, are scary, frightful,
But each time they are new.
The slightest thing makes me shed a tear as I cry in fear,
Waiting in silence until morning is near.

Another day. another day gone.
Every day we are moving on!

Kelly Whistance (12)
King Henry VIII School, Abergavenny

Why?

Why are we living?
Why are we here?
Why do we have mums
And dads?
Why do we have
Annoying brothers and sisters?

Why do we have planets?
Why do we have a moon?
Why do we have animals
And lots of other things too?
Why does the Earth have
Living people?
Why is the world so big?
Why do we have night and day?

Why . . .
Why . . .
Why . . .?

Alex Tipping (12)
King Henry VIII School, Abergavenny

The Battlefield

The rapid fire of the machine guns,
The screaming of the injured,
The tanks run through the battlefield,
Shooting, bleeding, dying.

The wives at home are crying,
While men at war are dying,
The things we see are horrible,
War, horrid war.

What's the point of war
When we could just have peace?
Why should we risk our lives?
Why do we have to die?

Aled Jones (12)
King Henry VIII School, Abergavenny

The Life In Hurricane Katrina

At night in the dark
I could feel the Earth shaking
I was quaking

I thought it must be a dream
So I slapped myself
Then poured water over my head

Then I was soon to realise
It wasn't a dream
So I went to bed and pulled over the covers

Then I heard a rumble and tumble
I looked out of the window
My car was smashed and my roof was torn off

In the morning I looked back out of the window
I saw the devastation
So now I'm homeless

I thought to myself, *why me?*
Then I thought
It *wasn't* just me.

Josh Coulton (12)
King Henry VIII School, Abergavenny

The Weather

I wake up in the morning
Just as the day dawning
When the frost is crisp and fresh
No footprint is yet visible
And the weather is not miserable
My freezing breath escapes, to climb
Exciting heights and then decline
The wind sweeps by like a cheetah after its prey
And the snow comes to lay
And make a white sheet on the ground.

Rhiannon Sheppard (11)
King Henry VIII School, Abergavenny

The Meaning Of Life

Life is but a feeling,
Of how easily it can break.
War, suffering and poverty,
How much can we take?
Will anyone answer my question,
What is the meaning of life?

To see Mother Earth's creations,
Or have the glory of love.
Parents who can care for you,
Or a faith in a being above?
Will anyone reply to my question,
What is the meaning of life?

Grieving, crying, laughing,
Emotions, confusion, despair.
Is it to feel these strange feelings?
Some of which you can hardly bear.
Will anyone respond to my question,
What is the meaning of life?

If you think deeply,
Unlock your great mind.
Imagine my question,
Imagine an answer.
Does anyone know the answer to my question,
What is the meaning of life?

Alex Williams (11)
King Henry VIII School, Abergavenny

The Dreaded Walk

As I make that walk every day
It never seems to get shorter
I walk and walk, faster and faster
But never get any further.

I fear who I may see
I feel my heart pumping
I feel it in my throat
Then I see them.

It started off just taking money
But then it got physical
A push, a poke
A nudge, a punch.

I can see the school
Should I run or should I take it?
They shout, I scream
But nothing comes out.

I fall
I think I just fainted
I see them running away
Someone is coming to help.

I can't tell anyone
Because they'll come for me
I want to go home, I feel sick
I can't tell.

I spoke to the nurse
She could tell something was wrong
She helped, she spoke to the Head
And now I don't get bullied.

Abigail Sadler (11)
King Henry VIII School, Abergavenny

Animal Rights

Hi, I'm Jack the fox,
My daddy was called Locks.
I say was because poachers came one day,
And Daddy got shot as he was lying in the hay.

The poachers shot him and then walked away,
There was nothing else Daddy could do.
I wish I was human,
To speak my mind,
True!

I would say, 'Hey, look you humans, we have feelings too,
How dare you treat us badly, when all we want to do is,
Live happily not sadly.'

I would speak for the other animals,
Give them a voice too.
Let them show their feelings,
Their fears and what they would do.

Poachers *can* find fun somewhere else.
You don't need a gun or a knife,
Just someone special with you all through
Your life!

Georgia Davies (12)
King Henry VIII School, Abergavenny

My Dog

My dog is a black Labrador,
Whom we all adore,
She thinks she can talk,
When she asks to go for a walk.
She runs around the park,
Occasionally stopping to bark,
She loves my dad's armchair,
But all my Mum does is complain about the hair!

Ruth Cochrane (12)
King Henry VIII School, Abergavenny

Words

Words, words everywhere, some bad, some good,
Some good, some bad.
Why do people get bullied?
Why do some people die?
So many questions, so little answers.

Words, words everywhere, some bad, some good,
Some good, some bad.
If I could not speak I'd be helped.
Only if people helped others.

Words, words everywhere, some bad, some good,
Some good, some bad.
If I turned back time, I'd not come here.
I know I've done bad things, I don't need to be bullied.

Words, words everywhere, some bad, some good,
Some good, some bad.

Charlotte Jones (12)
King Henry VIII School, Abergavenny

The Tiger

The tiger is orange
The tiger is orange and black
The tiger is orange and black striped
The tiger is orange and black striped with blue eyes
The tiger is orange and black striped with crystal-blue eyes
The tiger is orange and black striped with crystal clear,
                              blue eyes and a long tail.
The tiger is orange and black striped with crystal clear,
                              blue eyes and a long stripy tail,
The tiger is orange and black striped with crystal clear,
                              blue eyes and a long orange stripy tail
The tiger is orange and black striped with crystal clear,
                              blue eyes and long orange and black stripy tail
                              This is a tiger!

Louise Powell (12)
King Henry VIII School, Abergavenny

Open Water Disaster

As I sail the open water
I think that every second makes it shorter
The sound of the waves that break against the bow
I think of my chickens and my sow
The race has made me a trembling wreck
As I walk along the empty deck
The only thing that shares my yacht
Is the telephone, it's all I've got
I race my yacht to save a friend
Before disaster's made the end
The keel is swinging from side to side
If it hits the boat my friend will die
He'll get in a safety raft to get on Ecover
And together we'll sail to the port at White Dover
The rescue is done and we are safe
My wife is glad and we need a shave!

Richard Taylor (11)
King Henry VIII School, Abergavenny

The Meaning Of Life

If life had a meaning what would it be?
To live or to die,
To love or to hate,
To forget or forgive?
The meaning of life will never be clear.
Forever wondering, why are we here?
Perhaps there is no meaning, but to die,
And this world around us is just a lie.
We will never know what to be,
We will never see what all this is for,
But no one can answer this unanswerable question,
So we will never know the meaning of life.

Owen Haslegrave (12)
King Henry VIII School, Abergavenny

The Football Match

As I walk into the stadium
The team are training in front,
The manager holds his hand up
And waves it frantically at me.

The training is now over
And the match is about to start.
The ref blows the whistle
And the crowd begins to roar.

At the end of the match
Giggs, Bellamy and Koumas score
The crowd once again scream
And the Irish fans go home sad.

The match was great
And the score was three-nil
Wales won and the stadium sprung
And no one went home without a smile.

Ryan Price (13)
King Henry VIII School, Abergavenny

The African Boy

Babies crying, parents dying
Moaning, groaning, sobbing, weeping
The smell of death all around us
I don't have the smallest crust

Body aching, stomach empty
Always, always, always thirsty
Tiredness creeps up on me
Suffering is all I can see

Why are you letting me starve?
Why are you letting me die?
You say you want to help
But is it all a lie?

Ned Bramley (12)
King Henry VIII School, Abergavenny

Passion And Pride Of Champions

The rush of adrenaline,
The scream of the crowd,
With fear rising,
As high as a cloud!

The shout for the ball,
The miss pass was made,
Running for survival,
And the smash that was laid.

Your legs start to ache,
Your blood gains a boiling tint,
You have to defeat them,
Hit! Smash! Sprint!
To crush their dream,
Of being supreme!

Ten minutes to go,
Let's give 'em a show,
That they'll never forget!

As the final whistle blows,
The beaten-up souls,
And hopes of living the dream,
Sink down to their knees,
And cry, 'Why God, please?'

They never stood a chance,
At beating us back,
From the tile we rightly deserve,
We're the Ystrad Mynach team,
We'll always live the dream,
And be champions all,
Now and forever, standing tall.

Owen Dare (14)
Lewis School, Pengam, Bargoed

London

Welcome to my homeland,
There's a tour in it for you,
We don't greet with sea and sand,
Just a friendly 'How do you do'.

First of all it's Paddington Station,
To meet the bear from Peru,
The very heart of the British Nation,
Is waiting just for you.

Moving on to Mayfair,
Where rich folk tend to dwell,
American embassy's over there,
From Monopoly you can tell.

Next on the list is Baker Street,
As Gerry Rafferty knows,
The famous man we will meet,
Is known as Sherlock Holmes.

The Cenotaph is standing tall,
Glory in its wake,
We honour the men who gave it all,
Freedom's what they make.

Near Parliament Square is the House itself,
There dwell Commons and Lords,
Six hundred years of the country's wealth,
Won by shield and sword.

The city, it's here for you to visit,
Anytime you like,
The life, the people and the spirit,
Here it will all unite.

Rhys Owens (14)
Lewis School, Pengam, Bargoed

What Can I Do?

What can I do? What can I do?
I don't know, someone give me a clue.
I'm doing a poem. I don't know what to write,
I don't even know if it's wrong or it's right.
I don't know how to do this stuff,
I'm really annoyed, I have had *enough!*
Count to ten and calm down,
Because right now I look like a clown.
My paper is even laughing at me,
'You can't do it, hee, hee, hee!'
I can't seem to get it right,
It's not as easy as flying a kite.
Think of something fast, *write something down!*
Or smash the window and get out of town.
I am going to scream if I can't do this,
I wish I could get some help from Miss.
Oh cool, looks like I have got a clue,
Now this is my poem from me to you.

Alex Williams (14)
Lewis School, Pengam, Bargoed

Welsh Wonders

Where the sheep graze
Where the tourists gaze
Where the rivers flow
That's where I want to go

See the giant mountains
See the water fountains
See it covered in snow
That's where I want to go

Taste the salty sea air
Looking at the rockpools with their wear and tear
Listening to the sea,
Just you
        and me.

Nathan Hazell (13)
Lewis School, Pengam, Bargoed

The Simpsons

It starts off with a song,
The video makes you laugh each time,
Every time it's different,
But there is no rhyme.

There's Bart, Lisa and Homer,
There's Marge, Maggie and Otto,
There's Burns, Millhouse and Flanders,
And Barney, Krusty and Mo.

Homer is big and fat,
Lisa is not fat or thin,
Bart should fatter but,
Maggie could fit in a bin.

Homer's food is doughnuts,
Bart's food is junk,
Maggie's food is anything,
Lisa just plays the trombone for funk!

So these are the funny Simpsons,
Who live life to the max each day,
Do you think we should do it too
Or stick with a normal day? *Doh!*

Amar Ali (13)
Lewis School, Pengam, Bargoed

The Price

The battlefield is Britain,
Nowhere there is fine,
The rest of Europe has gone,
Blown up like a mine.

The battles take place in urban places,
Troops file in in tanks and planes,
Gunshots sound from the city centre,
Mortars fall, smash windowpanes.

Houses are taken,
One by one,
By resistance groups,
Till the battle is won.

The streets pile up with dead and dying,
Medics rush to help the wounded,
Blood pours from open wounds,
Then the victory is sounded.

An example has been set though,
A point has been made,
Make your way back home,
The price has been paid.

Ben Fussell (16)
Lewis School, Pengam, Bargoed

Bikes

I love biking, me.
Try different types, mountain, skate park,
I love it when me and my mates
Just go out on our bikes.

My bike's a stunner,
All stealth, black and nasty,
But not nasty to me though,
I haven't fallen off it yet!

I'd love to live at the top of a mountain,
So I could ride down it every day,
On my way to school,
Except on Saturdays!

Flying down the track,
Mud flicking in your eyes,
The smell of sweat rising quickly,
Drenching your T-shirt.

I love biking, me.

Liam Shaughnessy (14)
Lewis School, Pengam, Bargoed

What's The Point?

Nations vs nations
Battling all in vain
Countless deaths by millions
Inflicting, adding pain

What if we joined hands
And cleared up this wreck?
So stubborn and hard-minded
No one will accept!

Millions of innocent lives
Ruined by greed
Swallowed up in politics
Tell me, where is the need?

Elders may be wise
And war is such a threat
But youngsters must ensure
Peace on Earth is met!

Ieuan Protheroe (16)
Lewis School, Pengam, Bargoed

Nothing

I am thinking of nothing
All is blank
I know what would be good
An empty thought bank?

A jar on my shelf
Full of good thoughts
Helping me when I'm blank
I called the jar blank.

The doctor says I'm off my head
I don't care this bank is mine
And it doesn't cost even a dime!
And it's all mine, mine, *mine!*

People try to steal my jar
But I hide it in my car!
Nobody can touch my jar
Cos I know how to drive this car!

Lee Knicz (13)
Lewis School, Pengam, Bargoed

Death

A man is lying in his bed,
He knows for sure that he'll soon be dead.
He struggles,
He fights,
Well into the night,
But in the end Death will come calling.

A woman is crying by the bed,
She is terrified of where he might tread.
She sobs,
She weeps,
Until she falls asleep,
And in the end Death comes calling.

Death is almighty,
Death is all-consuming,
You can't escape,
So don't be assuming.

Ryan Lintern (13)
Lewis School, Pengam, Bargoed

The Bully

I am walking through an alley
and I hear a noise
I turn around sharply
and I see some boys.

They have a gun in their hand
I don't know if it's real
and I haven't done anything
so what is the deal?

They tell me it's fake
and want to be friends
They now want me to spot someone
that is round the bend.

I go round the bend and see . . .
a huge boy
He's almost unreal
he looks like a toy.

He goes to punch me
and I hear a bang
He was shot in the head
by the gang.

You said it was fake
you lot are liars
I wish you to Hell
and burn in the fires.

David Shenton (14)
Lewis School, Pengam, Bargoed

Worth

Look around and see the family
The family stares back in their patronising sorrow
No one cares, I am just a number
Just pound signs on the eyes of my loved ones.

The monotonous beep reflects the beat of my lonely heart
The family still watching, waiting, wanting.
I am urged not to shut my eyes
But why shouldn't I? It's what they really want.

I go weak and see the family and their expressions
What is my worth?
Love, passion and emotion? Or,
House, car and account?

Breadwinner or lottery winner
Everyone's just the same
What is the worth of emotion?
What is the worth of my love?

One week and I shall placed whence I came
Into the ground
Marked by a concrete slab
Marked by a passing thought.

James Fletcher (15)
Lewis School, Pengam, Bargoed

Loveless, Lifeless

Love has no place
In this world of sorrow.
The life of today
Is the death of tomorrow.

Happiness is nothing
And sadness grows vast.
Everything leaves
Because nothing can last.

Family, friends, loved ones,
Nothing can stay.
Even you're destined to go
Even if not today.

Love has no place
In this place of sorrow.
Because nobody cares
And everything is hollow.

Craig Evans (15)
Lewis School, Pengam, Bargoed

Street Life

Walking down the street like a gangster boy
Passing those people who we always annoy
A hood on our head, disguising our face
People walk past saying, 'What a disgrace.'

We drop our left legs as we walk on by
We make little kids scream and cry
A mother comes out with an angry face
We throw her a look - *don't invade our space.*

We share a can of beer
Smoking all the gear
Then the cops appear
We run in fear!

Jack Bradshaw (12)
Lliswerry High School, Newport

Newport Poem

Newport is not an ordinary place,
Filled with nature,
Filled with people,
Weather changing and changing,
Sun risen up in the sky,
Then the sun fallen to sunset,
Stars sparkle in the sky,
Light dots lighting up the sky.

Children happy and cheerful,
The way people like it,
Rivers going by swiftly,
The water crashing the rocks,
Like beating up someone,
Cars go as fast as electric wires,
Old, ancient houses,
Like in the 1890s.

Newport has grown to a town, then to a city.
Delicious food from restaurants,
At night the moon appears,
Ghosts from the ground,
Hunting like cavemen,
Vampires at midnight,
Looking for fresh blood,
People ill,
Or people better,
No matter, at least they're living
Somewhere,
Good old Newport.

Pritesh Patel (11)
Lliswerry High School, Newport

Love, I Hate It

Love, love, it's horrible,
Buy gifts and boys get rubbish gifts,
Girls get expensive gifts,
Exchanging gifts,
Me sitting alone in the corner,
Watching, but none for me,
Love, the hugging and kisses,
I feel so sick but still watching,
I walk away, saying 'Hi' to my friends,
Friends who are the same as me,
No love for me and I give none.

Family are my love,
But only them,
Friends are my mates.
I hate love.
I don't know who loves me,
If that's true.
I hate people who spend too much on gifts,
And the others who don't.

Sam Berrecloth (12)
Lliswerry High School, Newport

My Day At The Seaside

The glistening sapphire ocean,
Sparkled in the sun.
The waves washed over my feet
As I began to run.

The seagulls screeched above my head,
The candyfloss smelt sweet,
My feet sank in the golden sand,
When I sunbathed in the heat.

I saw a kite soaring high,
Over the deep blue sea,
Held by a boy and father,
His age about three.

Down by the rock pool
There were tons of shells but two were special
In a way they reminded me of bells.

The day was drawing to an end
As the sun began to sleep,
The clouds seemed to disappear
Like little, lost sheep.

Adrienne Harris (11)
Lliswerry High School, Newport

A Poem For The Ages

This isn't the best of all poems,
The rhyming scheme doesn't quite work.
Not all the sentences really fit in;
Ms Middleton will go berserk!

The punctuation is awful,
The layout is rubbish as well.
My printer keeps printing things wonky,
And my black ink is giving me hell!

But setting these minor faults aside.
I still haven't told you why
This poem is so important
To all of your day-to-day lives.

You see, even though it's atrocious,
I tried the hardest I could
To come up with a poem
That at least a few folks thought was good.

So if you try your very best
And come up with something quite bad,
At least you'll know you did all you could;
You gave it all the effort you had.

And if the outcome is brilliant,
It paid off to try you see?
You should be really chuffed
That someone likes you over me . . .
Unlikely!

Rhysian Jones (14)
Maesydderwen Comp School, Ystradynlais

Along The Beach

Galloping along the beach,
wind in my hair.
Just me and my pony,
a beautiful Arab mare.
We're jumping in the waves,
playing in the sea.
Now the sun is setting,
and it's just my pony and me.

Natalie Clare Powell (14)
Maesydderwen Comp School, Ystradynlais

The Children Of Spring

The sun is rising over the hill
The lambs are sleeping calm and still
The wind is blowing the wild daffodil
I can hear the birds singing in the tree where I sit
The melody of the swallow and blue tit
The lambs are waking to the light of day
Gorging on grass and bundles of hay
Horses are now galloping, screaming neigh
I can smell the bees making honey
On this day that is so sunny
I pick an apple from the tree
The apple is sweet and makes me feel free
A lamb falls over and I scream, hee, hee
A bird takes her chick under her wing
And starts to sing
These truly are the children of spring.

Andrew Abdulla (12)
St Cyres School, Penarth

The Recipe Castle

A sprinkle of some excitement,
a dash of entertainment,
a teaspoon of enjoyment,
cook a cup full of love,
and stir with passion,
to make a recipe for an amazing life.

Throw in a castle,
and add a few dragons,
heat it all up,
and serve with a drizzle of myths, tales and legends,
a boiling temper
and with a chop up of firing balls.

A half gram of kings,
with the sizzling minutes,
a bang of surprises,
marinade in faith,
and when the knights come,
they can't help but mix in.

The knights will defeat the dragon,
by mixing a little bit of daffodils,
just don't overcook the dragon,
or it will pour gallons of mud on you.

Charlotte Sabal (11)
St Cyres School, Penarth

I Am The Boy

I am the boy
Who cannot see

I am the boy
Whose name is Lee

I am the boy
Whose name is Fright

I am the boy
Could you turn on the light?

I am the boy
Who walks alone

I am the boy
Who's on his own

I am the boy
Who can only feel

I am the boy
Whom no one can heal

I am the boy
Who cannot see

I am the boy
Whom people can't see.

Josh Dutfield (12)
St Cyres School, Penarth

Snowboard

Hello, I am Board and this is the story of me,

I was a long and wide piece of birchwood,
Then I was cut into a thick ski,
OK, everything was going quite well by this time,
I was placed in between Boardy and Boardo,
We were like ham, tomato and lettuce in a sandwich,
I was burnt to bend my two ends,
So I was the core of the snowboard.
Other materials were added to finish me off,
I heard them say a snowboard should always be strong.

OK, I think we're ready.

I could just peek out of the snowboard,
And I saw a boy putting on all the protective clothing,
He was wearing a helmet and elbow and kneepads,
And then he was ready to go.

OK, we're ready.

He got strapped to me and off we went,
Oh no, this was a goofy,
I was now facing down the slope,
I thought he was quite good, no, he was very good,
He was steering me like a rudder on a boat.

OK, we're ready.

He got strapped to me and we were off,
I was facing down hill and suddenly
He jumped off a huge ramp and he landed safely.

OK, now we're definitely ready.

A while on and Jamie Philip is a professional and I am still his
snowboard,
I am speeding down the slope in a race in the Winter Olympics,
All I hear is, 'Jamie Philip has won.'

This is me, Board, and this is the story of me!

Tasmin Pickford (13)
St Cyres School, Penarth

The Clearer Picture

I am a wall strewn with tears,
That have been caused by their peers.
It will sound like a story, but surely it's not,
Because what I will be telling you is a lot.
It will start on your first day,
They will hate you and tell you to go away,
Give a hit, call you a name,
Then they start to give you the blame.
It will put you in the blues and
They will make up all your rules.
You will feel sad,
And they will be glad,
To see that they will make your life hell
By taking your stuff to make you yell.
Stand up now, push them back,
Tell them how you want your life back.
Then now tell them they are a cow,
Then shout at them, 'Stop it, now!'
Days after that, now it's stopped, the person has a happy face.
Has never wanted to remember that nasty place,
Because they are happy,
But how about you?
Stand up now, put them back
And get your life back on track.

James Griffiths (12)
St Cyres School, Penarth

Why Me?

I feel so bad,
I hate those bullies,
They make me feel sad,
There's only one thing I can say,
Why me?

They call me names,
They chase me around,
They think it's all games,
There's only one thing I can say,
Why me?

I try to hide,
But they always find me,
Even though I try and try,
There's only on thing I can say,
Why me?

Eventually I blurted it out,
The teacher was shocked,
She sorted it all out,
Now it's all over,
There's only one thing I can say,
Why me?

I can hang out with friends,
Now my life's back,
Now I'm not at wits' end,
There's only one thing I can say,
Why me?

Samantha Lemmer (13)
St Cyres School, Penarth

Empty Shells

Leaving one life is beginning another,
they go together like days and nights,
like the roots of a tree and its fruits,
like empty shells
in the steel blue sands of twilight
when the near-full moon casts an eye
and a vagrant tide washes the soles
of my feet.

Leave softly, but leave -
then will you be complete
as you touch and receive
the rising moments
in their unabashed splendour -
and allow all fear in your heart
to dissolve forever.

Are we not then like these
tiding shells
that gather on beaches
buffeted by the waves,
polished and refined in the depths?

Wandering the vast sea
we arrive, yes
we arrive in one majestic breath on the shores
of freedom
to cease at last, to rest
smiling jewels
discreetly reflecting
the un-nameable silence.

Raviell Gehlan (11)
St Cyres School, Penarth

The Outsider

I'm an outsider,
I'm all alone.
No one will love me
Or give me a home.

I'm an outsider,
I'm a stranger,
When I look at the sky,
All I see is a big lie.

I'm an outsider,
Happy or loved? I'm neither.
I'm as sad as a dark night,
Please shed me some light!

I'm an outsider,
I'm not much brighter
Than any other person.
I'm a part of exclusion.

I *am* an outsider,
I'm all alone.
No one will love me
Or give me a home.

Veronica Andrade (13)
St Illtyd's RC High School, Cardiff

Empty

I sit here all alone
Waiting for the phone
No one calls every day
I wish I could just fade away

Alone, abandoned and unloved
I wish someone would come from up above
With darkness all around
I wish I could be found

They taunt and they hate me
Why won't they let me be?
I hope one day they'll realise
That I'm one of the good guys

I have never, ever spoken
I wish I had never been awoken
I want love to be near
But I'm hidden in fear

How did this all start?
It's breaking my heart
I want rid of this pain
Never to be felt again

This is the last entry
Of a girl who is empty . . .

Kelly Tsakiris (14)
St Illtyd's RC High School, Cardiff

Outsiders

Outsiders are loners, they do not belong;
Outsiders are weird, they like the saddest of things,
Outsiders are stupid, they cannot see the things that are cool,
Outsiders are sick, how can they like that rubbish?

Outsiders are *not* loners,
        they are alone because the real outsider made them,
Outsiders are *not weird*,
        they are told they are by the real outsiders,
Outsiders are not *stupid,*
        they are brave to be different from the real outsider,
Outsiders are not *sick,*
        the real outsider is!

The real outsider is *not* who you think,
The real outsider is *not* uncool,
The real outsider is *not* thought to be one,
The real outsider is *not* the one feeling the pain!

The real outsider is the one at the top,
The real outsider is the one who is different,
The real outsider if the one who makes the decisions,
The real outsider is the one who is not a nice person!

I am glad I am not the real outsider, are you?

Pepe Schiavo (14)
St Illtyd's RC High School, Cardiff

Standing Outside

Standing outside
Feeling the cold through the soles of your shoes
Watching them smiling
Wondering what it feels like
That happiness thing

Crying inside
Feeling the pain in the depths of your heart
Watching them laughing
Suffering each giggle
As a wound to the soul

Walking away
Feeling more alone than ever
Remembering their faces
As they sat there
Talking

You are an outsider
Only dreaming of their life
Pretending you fit
Like you're not just
Scum on their shoes

Pretending you're not an outsider.

Rebecca Smith (14)
St Illtyd's RC High School, Cardiff

Lie About Lenny

I'm cold and lonely,
tired and hungry, all these
things people take for granted.
No one has stopped to say
hello, no one has come to help.

My name is Lenny, the loafing lie-about
but really I'm just Lenny, hungry, grumpy
and cold.
Here I am now begging for money,
damn you smell funny, that's all the
working man has to say to me, the outsider,
lie about Lenny.

Conor Driscoll (14)
St Illtyd's RC High School, Cardiff

The Pollution Man

The pollution man has an eco system maths house.
The air has windy travels.
The water, the European Union and the Commonwealth
of Independent States have
become eco-friends and the system wants to shut down
and they all live happily
ever after. The night before the call of the sting.

Mustafa Abdi (13)
Sybil Elgar School (NAS) Southall

Evanescent

We await our doom
Yet we hold our head high.
Laughter, jokes and happiness
Even though our time is nigh.

We've been left here,
Like unwanted clothes,
Given to a charity,
(About which nobody knows!)

Life passes us by
Like so many fears
Cried for the pain
That, long ago, a cut once hurt.

The days crawl on
Like a weary explorer
Memories leave us like
Ever-evanescent people.

Srishh Jean Baburaj (14)
The Ash Technology College, Ashford

You Could Have Saved Me

When you picked on me I would cower in a corner,
because I am a nobody.
I would walk in the playground alone,
because I have nobody.

You could have saved me with your companionship,
but you chose to exclude me.

I'm neither black nor white,
yet you would discriminate me.
I had no sense of pride or self-worth,
and you used that to your advantage.

You could have saved me with your kind words,
instead you bombarded me with abuse.

When I was as low as could be,
you found a way of kicking me even lower.
And when I tried to get back up,
you pushed me back down.

You could have saved me with a helping hand,
in spite of this you decided to join in with the others.

When I tried to take my life,
you called me an emo and an attention seeker.
Yet when I lived,
you called me a waste of space.

You could have saved me by giving me a reason to live,
but you didn't.

I could be neither happy nor sad,
dead or alive.
I could never win with you,
or even lose with dignity,
no one would accept me and I had no place to call home.

You could have saved me!

Amie Krubally
The Ash Technology College, Ashford

Roz

I miss her, I really do
It's only been a day or two,
But it feels like forever,
I spent the day with my parents,
But really I was with her.
Holding her hand, feeling her hugs,
I could feel her touch so clearly.
At least, I wanted to so deeply,
I wish she'd call, I'd wish she'd say,
Everything's going to be okay.
I need to hear the magic words,
From her voice, that makes me sway.
I suppose I should be smiling, laughing,
And being grateful too.
I'm the only person who'll hear her say
'I love you'.

Michael Murphy (15)
Willows High School, Cardiff

Lonely Love

There in the corner, so lonely and still,
Thinking about her heart, climbing a hill,
Trying to reach the top, to her one true love,
But her heart is stopped, by someone up above.

Why has the heart stopped?
As an emotional tear is dropped!
She just wants the world to see her love,
Her love for him is as white as a dove.

She can't face the world that's keeping them apart,
While she has an incomplete heart.

Hannah Smith (14)
Willows High School, Cardiff

The Seven Ages Of Life

(Inspired by 'As You Like It')

My poem is about the seven ages of life,
But take time to read it, it won't cause you strife.

Firstly it's a baby,
Who looks lonely and blank,
One day this bold child,
Will drive a huge tank

Second a boy who dawdles to school,
Puts on an interested face, but who can he fool?
He wants to move, get on with his life,
Soon he will be thinking about having a wife.

The time has come for this young lover,
To buy a house away from his mother.
To live in harmony, happily ever after,
And have fun hearing his children's laughter.

Oh no, what's this? He's gone to war!
His body's cold and his joints are sore.
There are gun shells and debris flying through the air,
Whizzing past his short brown hair.

He's middle-aged now; he's had lots of fun,
He's settled down, lying in the sun,
Thinking about the good times that he has had,
Good memories that won't make him sad.

He's a pensioner now, his joints are weak,
The slightest bend and the joints start to creak,
He rattles his brain, thinks about the good things he has done,
These past eighty years have been so much fun.

He's dead now and sadly missed,
His grandson was the last person he kissed,
He hopes and hopes that he won't be dim,
And follow good ways just like him.

Jake Niersmans (14)
Willows High School, Cardiff

Don't Fear The Reaper

The maddened form was seething,
His hair an unruly mess.
The house around was crumbling,
The news, shocking nonetheless.

He clambered down the stairs,
With his stick to guide the way,
He seemed almost robotic,
The strangers didn't want to stay.

They watched him coming nearer,
His face came into view,
His painted mouth was smiling,
But his black eyes showed the truth.

The two brothers waited,
For they knew of his power,
The older boy, Dean, stepped forward
Though he felt much like a coward.

The younger brother bit his lip,
His face set in a frown.
As he remembered his nightmare,
Of that very same clown.

Dean put his arm out,
Holding him back.
For it was he the clown wanted,
To get his own back.

Then the figure deteriorated,
Leaving ash in his way.
The brothers sighed deeply
As they realised they were okay.

When they thought about it after,
They realised with a start,
When told 'Don't fear the reaper',
You should follow your heart.

Jessica Ackerley (12)
Ysgol Bryn Alyn, Wrexham

Under The Stairway

Under the stairway something lies,
With fierce, bloodshot demon eyes.
But yet it sits there day by day,
Watching.

Many people walk past there,
They know something is under there,
But yet it stands there day by day,
Watching.

Although this thing is watching there,
They scream as it comes out to scare,
This thing now comes out day by day,
Grabbing.

Little kids play by there,
And watch that thing under the stair,
And yet it comes out day by day,
Snatching!

Melissa Siân Jones (12)
Ysgol Bryn Alyn, Wrexham

Forever Lady Elizabeth

Forever watching
Forever listening
Never falling
Always standing
Forever shall I be the Lady Elizabeth!

She locks me away
So not to be seen
Away from the eyes
That want to be free
Forever shall I be the Lady Elizabeth!

They try to make me speak
What do they want me to be?
Much is expected of me
Nothing proved can be
Forever shall I be the Lady Elizabeth!

Forever shall I be the Lady Elizabeth?

Hannah Biggerstaff (14)
Ysgol Bryn Elian, Colwyn Bay

World War III, Planet Zulu

Stop! Drop and roll!
Hide behind that Hummer truck
Stop! Drop and roll!
Be careful that you don't get stuck.

Planet Zulu, what ya gonna do?
What ya gonna do
When we come for you?

We are like the Zorgon dwellers
We are gonna get you
With our finest fellas!

Laser guns, bazooka 3,000s
What ya gonna do?
We want your planet!
Yes we do!

This is a world war
Winner takes all!
If you get shot
Then you'll take a nasty fall.

We'll do a drive-by
In our rocker Hummer.
We'll pop your back tyre
Oh, what a *bummer!*

Hooray, hooray, Zulu is ours
You'd better bow down
To our
Super rocket power!

Stop. Drop and roll!
Hide behind that Hummer truck
Stop! Drop and roll!
Be careful you don't get stuck!

Tristan Rowllings (12)
Ysgol Bryn Elian, Colwyn Bay

Memory?

Memories . . .
Who can remember
Things that seem
So far away
To pull them out
From outer space

How important
Amazing things
Happen
Then disappear

We can't change
What's happened back there
In the back of our mind
Just there

Horrible as it may seem
Harder than we can bear
There, there
Soft and quiet

What are they?
Little glints of the past
Buried deep under the Earth's crust
Lovingly delightful
Horribly vicious

Memories . . .
They are what you want. . .

Katie Mason (14)
Ysgol Bryn Elian, Colwyn Bay

Big Fat Rat

I once had a kitten
That was bitten
By a *big fat rat!*

The size was twice
It gave us a fright
And ate all of our cheese!

Traps we set
But to no effect
Enough we'd had of this rat!

Professionals we got
To put a stop
And slay this abnormal
Rat!

They set up traps
And gassed it out
They beat it with a stick

The fat rat died
For some reason we cried
The rat we loved like a son

We searched the attic
And to our surprise
We found ten baby rats!

So we kept them
And loved them
We bless that
Big fat rat!

Liam Evans (14)
Ysgol Bryn Elian, Colwyn Bay

With My Grandad

He had only weeks left
but he got out of bed
and walked with me
to the park.

I was five
or six and he walked with a stick,
unsteady.
Maybe I didn't notice at all
but I loved him so much
it just didn't matter.
I'm very glad we went.

The day was happy and smiling.
A bird would have sung in a tree.
It probably did.
But I wouldn't have heard,
I was full of childish pleasure.

I want that feeling back.
And it makes me wonder -

Is memory a bubble?
Perfect
till it pops?

That day was like a bubble.
Lovely
till it stopped.

Laura Williams (14)
Ysgol Bryn Elian, Colwyn Bay

Heaven's Kingdom

As I looked over what
I thought was my kingdom
My fans bowed down to me,
As the wind blew through their bristles,
Shaking off their little white gems.

As I looked over what
I thought was my kingdom,
The ground as I knew it was
Being re-laid with brand new
Glistening white crystals.
They fell into place and
Made the new carpet.

As I sat on what I
Thought was my throne,
I glided over the mountains
In my kingdom.

But is this my kingdom?
As I reached the end of my run,
A *man* stood in my route,
As I glided through him he crumbled.
I stood up and rolled him back into one piece.

As I looked over what I thought
Was my kingdom
My fans no longer bowed,
And their white crystals all melted
I stood up and thought . . .

My kingdom slipped through my fingers,
Wait till next year,
You know this
My kingdom.

Katie Owen (14)
Ysgol Bryn Elian, Colwyn Bay

The Pipe

We were playing with a ball,
But down the hole it did fall.

Motty was very brave,
And poo came out the wall.

I remember it, like it was yesterday,
By the sewer we did play.

Our tennis ball fell down the sewer,
We'd thought we'd call it a day.

But Motty said, 'I'll go,'
His braveness he was about to show.

As he climbed over the fence,
He was ready to go below.

On to the pipe he held,
And down the hole it fell.

Faeces poured out everywhere,
Oh, how awful was the smell.

Motty didn't know what to do,
The hole was filling up with poo.

We were laughing so hard,
Our yard smelt like a zoo.

Motty climbed over the gate,
And hid behind his mate.

As the poo was pouring out,
Motty ran for the gate.

Ryan Rowlands (14)
Ysgol Bryn Elian, Colwyn Bay

Will She Still Love Me? Says Teddy

My little baby cries,
Hugging me close, never to let me go.
I don't think she ever will. I hope.

My little baby, I love you so.

My baby girl growing to a walking, talking girl!
Chewing at my ears, loving me.
I don't think she'll ever stop. I hope.

My baby girl, I love you so.

My big girl, going to school. Already!
The years fly by.
She holds me high, then gently lets me down.
I don't think she will ever leave me. I hope.

My big girl, I love you so.

Katie Boughen (13)
Ysgol Bryn Elian, Colwyn Bay

Snow Day

We saw the snow falling down,
It started to stick as it hit the ground.

We listened to the radio to see if school was off,
I had to wrap up warm so I wouldn't get a cough.

We went up to Llysfaen to see my friend Paige,
We went in her house for warmth and watched the film 'Ice Age'.

We went sledging down the hill,
My top went up, I got a chill.

As it started to melt and the sky went dark,
We started walking back to the park.

Laura Jones (14)
Ysgol Bryn Elian, Colwyn Bay

Stalingrad

Above the Volga's still waters, in the late afternoon
The sky brought August birds with the darkening gloom
A thousand to soar, with their thundering roar
Above the city of Stalin.

In the smouldering skeleton, now merely a frame
Where death with its screams and its pain came to reign
And fires swept through, lit the nights muted blue
Some life still remained.

For in the streets, autumnal shell
As the bullets and bombs still plummeted from Hell
The Russians, outnumbered, shrinking and weakened
Refused to give in.

In the crumbling houses, between burnt-out rooms
Where soldiers, once enemies, found their tombs
As spilt blood spread in a crimson blush, before the hush
In the city of Stalin.

Sophie Kirkham (14)
Ysgol Bryn Elian, Colwyn Bay

I Hate That Stuff

Families separated,
Death's a major part of it.
War
I hate that stuff.

Animals suffering,
Babies suffocating.
Pollution
I hate that stuff.

People bruised,
It's always in the news.
Violence
I hate that stuff.

Drugs taken with them,
People can be cured with them.
Needles
I hate that stuff.

Always unfair,
Innocent pupils despair.
Class detention
I hate that stuff.

Green and slimy,
And shaped like a tree.
Broccoli
I hate that stuff.

Katie Liber (14)
Ysgol David Hughes, Menai Bridge

I Hate That Stuff

Death's the foremost part of it,
Buildings get destroyed by it,
War,
I hate that stuff.

Pain's the primary goal of it,
Families are torn apart by it,
Abuse,
I hate that stuff.

Teenagers get high with it,
Many will die from it,
Drugs,
I hate that stuff.

Starvation's one result of it,
Few like to face to truth of it,
Poverty,
I hate that stuff.

People's lives destroyed by it,
Many are terrified of it,
Disease,
I hate that stuff.

Children are force-fed it,
Animals served dead with it,
Sprouts,
I hate that stuff!

Ben Assinder (13)
Ysgol David Hughes, Menai Bridge

Away With Words

Animals, boys, flowers and noise,
I like these things,
Do you?

School, heights, dentists and mites,
I hate these things,
Your view?

Little brothers and bossy mothers,
Irritating things,
You agree?

Long lie-ins and biscuit tins,
Nice things,
You see?

Graves, ghouls and murky pools,
Scary things,
I think.

Sloppy kisses and happy wishes,
Comforting things
Wink, wink!

Lots of words, some absurd,
Describing things I like.

All these have occurred,
Telling others,
'Bout my life!

Caitlin McGonigle (13)
Ysgol David Hughes, Menai Bridge

I Hate That Stuff

People get annoyed with it
Trees are blown with it
Wind
I hate that stuff.

Animals are killed by it
People are scared by it
Hunting
I hate that stuff.

Lives can be haunted by it
Children are taunted by it
Bullying
I hate that stuff.

People die because of it
I feel sad when I look at it
Poverty
I hate that stuff.

People are hit by it
Lives are demolished by it
HIV
I hate that stuff.

Yes I hate that stuff
Torturing pain
I hate that stuff!

Laura Fisher (14)
Ysgol David Hughes, Menai Bridge

I Hate That Stuff

Some girls plaster themselves with it
Animals go through hell for it
Make-up
I hate that stuff!

People get killed in it
George Bush loves it
War
I hate that stuff!

People get addicted to it
Nothing is real in it
Soap operas
I hate that stuff!

Hair grows wild on it
My kitten tried to eat it
My brother's feet
I hate that stuff!

Everyone hates it
No one likes it
Cross-country
I hate that stuff!

Pregnant women are famous for it
There are always carrots in it
Vomit
I hate that stuff!

The Earth is being choked by it
Global warming is caused by it
Pollution
I hate that stuff!

Burgers are soaked in it
Some have a phobia of it
Fat
I hate that stuff.

Sophie Cooke (14)
Ysgol David Hughes, Menai Bridge

I Hate That Stuff

Children love to play in it
Worms like to squirm in it
Mud
I hate that stuff!

Addicts get killed by it
I can't stand the smell of it
Cigarettes
I hate that stuff!

Innocent lives are ruined by it
Idiots love the thought of it
War
I hate that stuff!

Most families are scared of it
My dad had to suffer from it
Cancer
I hate that stuff!

The sea is thickly coated in it
The Earth is slowly dying from it
Pollution
I hate that stuff!

Hospitals are stuffed with it
The elderly have had enough of it
Illness
I hate that stuff!

Children lose confidence over it
Parents can't see the point of it
Modelling
I hate that stuff!

Lauren Dixon (13)
Ysgol David Hughes, Menai Bridge

Away With Words

His name was Steve,
You'd never believe,

His hair was green,
Like a runner bean.

He'd talk all day,
In his mate's café.

He'd talk to the girls,
About their golden curls.

He'd chatter in tests,
He ignored the requests.

He was a likeable fella,
His girlfriend was Bella.

Bella was very vain,
She had a good brain.

The two lovebirds,
Were never lost for words!

Chatter, chatter, all day long,
Together they belonged.

Away with words,
Were the two lovebirds.

Until the day,
She ran away.

His name was Rex,
He had a BMX.

As thick as a brick,
As thin as a stick.

Steve no longer spoke of Bella,
He was no longer a lucky fella!

Amy Congrave (13)
Ysgol David Hughes, Menai Bridge

I Hate That Stuff

You get stung by it
Hot countries are full of it
Mosquitoes
I hate that stuff

Omega three is in it
Slimy, scaly and sickly is it
Fish
I hate that stuff

Landscape is ruined by it
People lose family by it
Earthquakes
I hate that stuff

Eyes hurt because of it
People can die by inhaling it
Smoke
I hate that stuff

I have never understood it
World devastation is caused by it
Terrorists
I hate that stuff

Families plummet into grief because of it
All ages can suffer from it
Cancer
I hate that stuff

Vinegar tens to hold it
Eyes squint from the sourness of it
Pickled onions
I hate that stuff.

Sophie Black (14)
Ysgol David Hughes, Menai Bridge

Away With Words

Away and away with words
We go, no stopping us now.

Away from the words of hate
Away with words of love.

Away from bad memories to
Recapture good and lost times.

Away from the pressure
Of drugs and fags.

Away and away we fly.

Away from the confusions
And the decisions.

Away from fears so strong they
Seems to drown us.

Away from the ordinary
To find the unique.

Away and away
Faster and faster we fly.

Away to find the perfect Heaven,
A place where no words need be spoken.

Away with words of hope and dreams,
We rise up high, soaring and flying.

Away to reach the perfect paradise,
Away to live and make a dream come true.

Gilda George (13)
Ysgol David Hughes, Menai Bridge

I Hate That Stuff

Winter brings loads of it
Dads break it
Wind
I hate that stuff

People soothe a bruise with it
I got knocked unconscious skating on it
Ice
I hate that stuff

Children build with it
Sandwiches taste awful with it
Sand
I hate that stuff

Ducks swim around in it
People run for cover from it
Rain
I hate that stuff

Pigs wallow in it
Football boots clog with it
Mud
I hate that stuff

Teachers give too much of it
Kids hate doing it
Homework
I hate that stuff.

Michelle Davies (14)
Ysgol David Hughes, Menai Bridge

Away With Words

Look deep into a child's eyes and what do you see?
One that can't speak is the hardest, you have to agree!

A child that has no emotions,
The child that can only stare into space.
The child that people bully,
Because they have no look on their face.

Are they thinking of the future?
Are they thinking of the past?
Are thy thinking of what will come to them?
Are they thinking of why their life isn't passing very fast?

Are they thinking of their favourite football team?
Are they thinking of their next holiday?
Are they thinking of their day at school?
Are they thinking of what they'd like to say?

If only they could speak,
And tell us what they're thinking.
Instead of making us guess,
And have to decide what they're thinking!

Their life just passes by,
Listening to people that think they're strange.
But what can they do about it,
They were born that way!

So think about it once,
Then think about it twice.
They can't change who they are,
So at least try to be nice.

Away with words,
Away with words,
Some people just don't know what it's like,
To be away with words!

Hannah Cole (14)
Ysgol David Hughes, Menai Bridge

Away With Words

When I sit alone and think
I remember times gone by,
I shake my head and heave a sigh,
And wonder how time flies.

But then I feel guilty
At how much time I put to waste,
All the time I lay in bed
Because of days I can't face.

That's when I wish I could go back
And spend my time again,
I think of things I wish I'd done,
Like spend more time with friends.

I'd sit on that hill a bit longer,
Lounging in the sun,
I'd laugh that little bit louder
And do things that needed to be done.

I'd jump in that puddle,
I'd swing on that swing,
I'd be carefree and happy,
And worry about nothing.

I'd smile at everyone,
I'd cheer louder for my team to score,
I'd eat that last piece of cake,
And run away with my words a bit more.

But times gone by are times gone by,
And we can't change a thing,
All we can do is keep memories dear,
And smile at what life brings.

Robyn Simone Wignall (13)
Ysgol David Hughes, Menai Bridge

Away With Words

Remember that time,
When I first saw your smile,
You walked over and talked for a while,
From that day on we've been good friends,
Good times, good times

Remember that year,
I went to Greece,
I went to the disco in my black dress,
Danced all through the night,
Good times, good times

Remember that day,
When I went to the park,
I had an ice cream just after dark,
It was so peaceful and calm,
Good times, good times

Remember that month
When I had my birthday,
We went in a limo, oh, what fun,
The cake was delicious,
Good times, good times.

Samantha Fleming (13)
Ysgol David Hughes, Menai Bridge

Shake Off The Stereotype

Chavs,
Hoodies and trainers,
Fags and foundation.

Goths,
Leather and make-up,
Jewellery and spikes.

Emos,
Death and self-harm,
Hairstyle and black.

Geeks,
High strapped bags,
And running to lessons.

Why are we stereotyped?
Why is it needed?
We are who we are!
Isn't that enough?

Break the stereotype!
Step into the light!
What's holding you back?
No one, that's right!

Elena Liber (14)
Ysgol David Hughes, Menai Bridge

Away With Words

Walking down the station platform,
Poisonous thoughts eat away at my mind,
I think of my mother and father.
I'm away with words of anger.

I sit down by a bench to catch a moment before I leave,
I wonder if I'm doing the right thing.
Confusion and fear drifts slowly back into place.
I'm away with words of fear.

My father's curses and banging bellow;
The sounds of Mother screaming.
I push the memories to the back of my mind.
I'm away with words of terror.

A door slams,
Father's gone.
I can't help myself - I am gone too.
I'm away with words of disbelief.

I begin to cry,
Hot tears trickle down my cheeks.
Has anyone noticed? I don't care now,
I'm away with words of grief.

The train is arriving at the station,
It is my last chance to turn back
But no . . .

I have been away with words of anger,
Away with words of fear,
Away with words of terror,
Away with words of disbelief,
Away with words of grief,
And now . . .

I shall go away with silent words.

Bronwen Llinos Evans (13)
Ysgol David Hughes, Menai Bridge

Away With Words

This poem's about a team
Called FC Words,
Who had never won a game,
All felt like nerds.

They were so crud,
All their managers quit,
They needed a manager,
And they needed one quick.

Then along came a guy,
Called Frankie Hurtz,
Who went and trained,
The team of FC Words.

Their next match was away to
Lancaster City,
Who had never lost a game
And were really quite dirty.

'I know you think you're crud,'
Said Frankie Hurtz,
'But you can win this
Without getting hurt.'

By half-time
FC Words were a goal down,
Frankie Hurtz was angry,
And the team all had frowns.

By the final whistle
FC Words had won it,
The score was 2-1,
Their confidence raised to a peak.

James Shambrook (14)
Ysgol David Hughes, Menai Bridge

Away With Words

As I attempt to write a poem
My thoughts begin to wander
Over golden sand and powder snow
There's no place where my thoughts cannot go

First my mind heads to the north
To lands of boundless ice
Where polar bears and Eskimos roam
Where Arctic foxes make their home

But the ice is melting
Along with the snow
The world is warming
And this is a warning

Sadly my thoughts head to the south
To warmer climes and quieter shores
Yet every other place I look
Are the signs of what *progress* took

With more and more speed
My mind travels across the globe
Searching for areas unspoilt
But the very atmosphere is soiled

The Amazon rainforest is shrinking
Many of its species lost
Even Britain is changing
With weather now greatly ranging

Away with words!
Now is the time for action!
We must repair what we've done
Before all, even we, are . . .

. . . gone.

Ross Elliston (14)
Ysgol David Hughes, Menai Bridge

Away With Words

Back in the days of endless fun,
Through the fields we would run.
Laughing, dancing, swinging, playing,
I wish it was those days in which I was staying.
Those times were so good,
In the meadows we stood,
So many words that could only just tell,
The story of my life, which has now turned to hell.

Away with words is just how I like it,
As I fly back to my childhood, to where it all started.

I remember those days which were all about me,
When my life was a diary and only I had a key.
Autumn, summer, winter, spring,
No matter the season, I'd appreciate everything.
I was so happy in those familiar days,
I wonder what's changed as my life's now in a haze.
When I felt an ache in my heart,
I would travel back to the very best part.

Away with words is just how I like it,
As I fly back to my childhood, to where it all started.

Now I sit alone in a small open house,
Nothing around but a tiny mouse.
This again reminds me of the sweet sight of home,
But there's no escape now, there's nowhere to roam.
As the sky darkens over and I start to feel old,
I think back to those days when nothing was cold.
The darting through forests and splashing through streams,
It's now nothing but an image, a fading memory.

Now the only way to get there is away with words,
I glide up above and look down on the world.

Molli Dean-Aston (14)
Ysgol David Hughes, Menai Bridge

Away With Words

I lie here day by day,
People peer in then look away,
I don't know what they're saying,
Sometimes I see them praying.

When they look down at me,
Their eyes seem full of misery,
Their testing and prodding is a pain,
But yet they do it, again and again.

They rush me down a narrow corridor,
Then they test and prod some more,
They bring me back to my small space,
And I can see it from her face.

As they look down at me I start to cry,
Then they look away as if they don't know why,
How I long to be up and out of this bed,
So that I can finally experience the joys ahead.

I know that there's something more,
Something else behind that door,
I remember that girl running free,
How I wish that girl could be me.

Sophie Marie Hughes (14)
Ysgol David Hughes, Menai Bridge

Away With Words

Ask the mother who gave birth to a stillborn,
Ask the child with the missing teddy,
Ask the neighbour who no longer has his wife,
All have lost something,
But can only redeem them with words.

Ask the child that's bullied at school,
Ask the wife whose husband's at war,
Ask the patient on the transplant list,
All awaiting something,
But all they get is words.

Ask the pupil in the middle of their exams,
Ask the author who can't take anymore,
Ask the editor of The Guardian,
All must see a lot of them,
These things are called words.

Tell the neighbour that lost his wife,
Tell the wife whose husband's at war,
Tell the mother of the stillborn,
We can't achieve everything,
But we can away with words!

Lara Wright (14)
Ysgol David Hughes, Menai Bridge

Away With Words

Away, away with words,
Get rid of them,
Lose them,
Away with words.

Away, away with words,
Flying away, soaring away,
Through deep blue sky,
Away with words.

Away, away with words,
Swimming away, cutting through the water,
Gliding through the calm ocean,
Away with words.

Away, away with words,
Get rid of them.
Lose them,
Away with words.

Myfanwy Sian Hughes (13)
Ysgol David Hughes, Menai Bridge

Away With Words

Take a moment to think of others,
We children brought up by widowed mothers,
Completing chores in the scorching heat,
Struggling to afford shoes for my feet.

I have no school to attend,
My bones are brittle, but I'm on the mend,
A broken arm is nothing to me,
My bones are showing, there's plenty to see.

The big mansions and the flash cars,
Being Hollywood's superstars,
None of this matters to me,
All I want is family . . .

No food, no drink,
No thought left for me to think,
No money, no home,
No family left to call my own.

Rhian Williams (13)
Ysgol David Hughes, Menai Bridge

War

'We have no choice!' the ministers say,
As a decision is made to go to war,
For glory, respect, to prove their power,
These are their reasons for going to fight.

They sit in their green leather chairs,
Arguing about what 'Great' Britain does next,
Their innocent country that tries to keep peace,
But now following the West to war in the East.

Against terrorism they say they fight,
But the oil underground is what they want,
Taxes rise to pay for training the troops,
But what is the cost of a human's life?

Questions are asked but history makes the circle,
War once more seems to be the *answer,*
The only thing we would change in history,
Repeated once more.

History cannot be changed,
But the future can,
Why don't politicians take time to look?
Look at the endless list of names,
Carved into stone, their blood soaked into the battlefields.
Mere memories of the horror of war, memories of men.

Rhys Owen (14)
Ysgol David Hughes, Menai Bridge

Away With Words . . .

Looking back on what used to be,
The memories only you can see.

The bad ones, the good ones,
The happy and sad ones.

Memories make us who we are,
Without them life would be quite bizarre.

They an image or thought that can last forever,
And that will not be forgotten whatsoever.

Memories structure our lives,
And keep our thoughts revived.

A memory can take something,
And make it into a million more things.

A memory can be shared with the world,
And still be found enjoyable by every boy and girl.

Memories come straight from the heart,
And of us they will always be a part.

Memories, memories, never forgotten,
Treasure them forever and they will never grow rotten.

Polly Dempsey (13)
Ysgol David Hughes, Menai Bridge

Away With Words

'Guilty!' declares the judge.
'But I'm innocent!' cries the man.
An unfair trial.
Away with words.

'Goal!' screams the commentator.
'Get in!' roars the crowd.
The footballer clenches his fist.
Away with words.

'I love you,' say the eyes of the dying man.
His wife weeps silently.
The gentleman's last breath.
Away with words.

The clown slips up.
The banana skin on the floor.
Laughter all around.
Away with words.

The cat purrs.
Rubs its head on the girl's knees.
She smiles.
Away with words.

The birds sing on a crisp morning.
The winter sun shines down.
Nature's sounds.
Away with words.

Tony Blair speaks in parliament.
But no action follows.
False promises.
Away with words.

Joseph Holding (13)
Ysgol David Hughes, Menai Bridge

Away With Words

When early in spring,
The forest stood still,
No creature dared to come out,
Before the sun rose softly over the hill.

The trees turned, brown to green,
Many changes occurred,
But few could be seen.

When summer's blue sky faded to grey,
And swiftly ended the shortened day.

The traps in the field were hidden by dust,
With a sound of clicking as they were covered in rust,
With no chance of the wildlife being able to run,
The huntsmen started shooting their guns.

When on an autumn morning,
Colourful leaves began to fade,
In the misty, chilly and frosty air,
All the woodland trees grew steadily bare.

When winter came it brought a blanket of snow,
And all went white and freezing cold.

That year I remember clearly,
Caught up in my memories.

The wind can whisper, howl and blow,
It can move a slip of paper or put out a fire's glow.

As the wind is the platform to carry my words,
To fly them up high, as it does for the birds.

Gaby Ludlam (13)
Ysgol David Hughes, Menai Bridge

I Hate That Stuff

Some pockets are filled with it
Side effects come with it
Cigarettes
I hate that stuff

Children cry over it
Families are broken by it
Divorce
I hate that stuff

People are driven to it
Depression is the cause of it
Suicide
I hate that stuff

Millions are dead because of it
Guns help the cause of it
War
I hate that stuff

Tombstones are built for it
Soon all of us will be made to face it
Death
I hate that stuff

I hope people rot in Hell for it
Cases are unsolved by it
Murder
I hate that stuff

Chickens manufacture them
It smells when you boil it
Eggs
I hate that stuff.

Elan Jones (13)
Ysgol David Hughes, Menai Bridge

Why

What is the meaning of life?
To love and find a wife?

What is the point of love?
Why not roam free like a dove?

What is the point of being free?
Why not settle down and smile with glee?

What is the point in smiling?
Why don't we frown, be depressing?

What is the point in frowning?
Why not express by speaking?

What is the point in expressing at all?
Why not pretend that you're one foot tall?

What is the point of pretending?
Why not be honest, start mending?

What is the point of being honest?
Why not live life trying to be free?

What is the meaning of life?
A question I've had to ask twice.

We live, we die,
Why?

Emily Kirkham (13)
Ysgol David Hughes, Menai Bridge

Away With Words

Let's destroy all words,
Letters, books and stories,
Demolish talking, texting and email.
Alphabet unused,
Away with words.

Be rid of lists, rules, instructions,
Chaos begins!
Many become silenced,
As communication ends,
Away with words.

Without words,
Stereotyping and discrimination will stop,
Without words,
The people unable to speak, no longer excluded,
Everyone becomes equal.
An ideal world?
Away with words.

If there were no words,
How would we describe emotions?
Full of feelings hard to explain,
Stories untold, memories forgotten,
Loneliness and frustration,
Away with words.

Nathaniel Gregory (14)
Ysgol David Hughes, Menai Bridge

Away With Words

Freak, ugly, loner,
It can't hurt you,
They're just words.

Hate, love, rejection,
Mess up your emotions,
They're just words.

Can't, won't, will,
Make you think,
They're just words.

Fear, courage, confidence,
Scare you, but
They're just words.

Honesty, lies, trust,
It's just people getting carried away,
Away with words.

Sophie Bebb (13)
Ysgol David Hughes, Menai Bridge

A Picture

This picture reminds me of a time that used to be.
This picture reminds me of a place I long to see.
I look at the hills,
I look at the shores,
I look at the night from the window sill.

The hour grows late and I can't help but stare
At this photo I see before me,
It almost fills the air
With its brilliance.

The picture's so clear,
The feeling's right,
It makes me so sad,
But I feel no fright.

Am I this pathetic,
To think that this means something?
Am I so useless,
To think this could be alright?

It helps me remember,
I remember now,
I can't quite place it
And I'm not sure how,
But it speaks to me.

My family, my loves, my hate, my life.
It's all here and with just one knife
I could end it all.
Make it go away?
Could it be so easy?

These colours start to fade.
This life is but a photograph,
An image of the past,
Reflecting upon an open window,
Or maybe it's just my imagination?

But whatever it is, it's making me drown,
Drowning in the ink of this picture,
The picture that speaks to me -
It speaks to me softly and touches my soul.
And it kills me inside to know
That I'm never going back to this place.

Olivia Smart (14)
Ysgol Dyffryn Teifi, Llandysul

Dreams

Dreams are precious
So hold on to them
For they will die in time
Like a no-winged bird that cannot fly
They are the inspiration in Man

Dreams are the future
They make decisions for some
And choose which path to take in life for
Others

One special man had a dream
His name was Martin Luther King
He inspired the whole of America
That whatever we look like we are all the
Same inside

Without any dreams
There would not be any technology
And probably we would be extinct
Which shows dreams are life.

Daniel Jardine (11)
Ysgol Dyffryn Teifi, Llandysul

A Night Poem

It is night
And the empty shadows of the world
Surround me
A void of nothing
An eerie silence is in harmony with
Darkness and twilight.

It is as if
At any moment
That this silence should come to
Rest
And it shows nothing
Sees nothing
Feels nothing
And dies away into the blackness
Of the night
The sounds of the forests and fields
Return.

The moonlight
Reaches out as it
Dances through the trees
Where
The owl watches
The owl watches
It's the dead of night
And all is silent now
Dawn breaks and the day passes
It is night
It is night.

Carwyn Thomas (11)
Ysgol Dyffryn Teifi, Llandysul

Daffodils

Yellow, orange, green,
Popping up from the hard ground.
Guess what it could be.

Blazes of sunlight,
Light the beautiful garden.
Guess what it could be.

Catches your eyes soon,
Shines amongst the green hedges.
Guess what if could be.

They have a trumpet,
It is some sort of flower.
Guess what it could be.

'I know what they are,
They're pretty flowers from Wales.
I guessed what they were.'

Cerian Fflur Colbourne (12)
Ysgol Dyffryn Teifi, Llandysul

Light Is . . .

A blanket of warmth
A light bulb
A pool of sunny delight
A field of joy
Happiness
The end of the tunnel
A cave of joy
The 12 o'clock sunshine
The beginning
Yellow paper
Bleached hairstyle
A smile
Light is everywhere!

Tom Williams (15)
Ysgol Glan y Môr Comprehensive, Burry Port

Secrets

It's a daily routine in that place,
That same stern look across his face.

Her alarm rings at quarter to eight.
She wakes up at seven and nervously waits.

'Breakfast time darling.' You'd think he was kind,
her mood saddens as she knows exactly what he's got in mind.

'You know what you have to do to earn this food,'
He repeatedly tells her as she stands in the nude.

He looks into her eyes,
Then winks at her.
After all, she is his little prisoner.

It's over.
That's it for another day.
A satisfied smile on his face as he buttons up his shirt and walks away.

A sickening feeling hangs over her head.
That awful room with that wretched bed.

She fakes a smile all day long.
She knows what happened this morning was terribly wrong.

She hates going back to the pain and the fear.
She looks up at the clock - the end of the school day is near.

This girl needs help.
She needs it fast.
She never knows which day will be her last.

How long can this abuse pursue?
She could get help if only somebody knew . . .

Siobhan Thomas (14)
Ysgol Glan y Môr Comprehensive, Burry Port

One Life

*(inspired by a series of headlines taken from the Onelife supplement of
The Independent, dated 24th February 2007)*

'New Departures' . . . dump the words from the page
'How to change your life for the better',
'Take the plunge', 'Prepare yourself for bigger things' . . . they rage
How much bigger do they get than tackling Avian flu or
                               dealing with climate change

'You need to have 100% commitment', to
'Steer a fresh course for a new lease of life',
Forget about gang culture then and economic meltdown,
Islamic terror, illegal immigrants, home-grown trouble and strife.

'What about here and now'.
The front page not the supplement.
Let's move *'Away from the ordinary',*
To a cause close to my heart.

Does anyone care about our men in Iraq
Or the cause for such action and strife,
Who are fighting for peace and democracy
In a land that has recognised no human rights?

At a time when the world seems in conflict
The greatest threats to our future existence,
The solution to all these is simply
Down to the actions of *Onelife.*

David Blewitt (14)
Ysgol Glan y Môr Comprehensive, Burry Port

Thirst

The world is tough and the world is cruel
money, oil and books for school.
Children suffer in Africa's pits,
while world governments go about their politics,
looking for ways to stop the pain
and let Africa breathe a breath of relief again.

Little Somoni is only five
and he spends his days with a pain in his side.
As the sun beats down with no mercy upon his face,
he looks to his brothers and sisters the same.
Little Somoni doesn't understand why the water he drinks
is full of sand, he can't quite grasp the way of the world,
for Somoni is only five and doesn't have time to learn.
He doesn't have time to learn for his life could be short
when disease runs rife through every well and thought,
this is why Somoni's life is hell,
when his killer could linger at the bottom of a well.
No clean water, he lives like an animal,
what can we do?
What difference can we make?
When human beings' lives are at stake?

So why do some people have such affluent lives,
while other people struggle to survive?
Are we so different that we deserve better lives,
food, water and medicine to keep everyone alive?

Driving fast cars and going on holidays are things we do every day,
do you give a thought when we are burning theses gases
and oils away?
Killing crops,
ruining lives,
another bullet from the gun of the global warming rise.
Another few years and few more degrees,
and Africa's fate shall certainly be sealed.

So the message of my poem is, think,
and every time you pour clean water to drink,
spare a thought for children like Somoni first
and think of their everlasting thirst.

Gareth O'Reilly (15)
Ysgol Glan y Môr Comprehensive, Burry Port

The Discovery

For hours and hours,
I ponder in my thoughts.
Crossing out subjects,
That I believe are flawed.

After many hours pass,
I give up and search for guidance.
I surf the Web,
Study books and even
Ask for advice.

After discussion with family members,
A discovery overwhelms my mind.
I then proclaim out loud;
What a grand idea,
But will it work on paper?

I compare this new discovery
To previously pondered thoughts.
With great happiness and joy,
I find this obliterates them all.

With this new idea
Playing havoc in my mind,
I try my best to structure it,
And with success I find
I have finally written my design.

Robert Bathgate (15)
Ysgol Glan y Môr Comprehensive, Burry Port

Only He

He was the cause for all of this madness
Bringing us grief and causing us sadness
Sending our loved ones out into battle
Without enough food to face the gun's rattle
He was the one, yes he, only he
The only one mad enough to hurt you and me
We all know the one who caused all this pain
One man, Adolf Hitler who was quite insane

He took away families, slaughtered, maimed and much more
Until all the world was forced into war
But they were quite lucky, as for the Jews you see
Were considered inhuman and were tortured by he
Into making you think that he, only he
Could make this whole planet the way he thought it should be
But the only thing I saw were the remains of the dead
With bodies and faces all coloured blood-red

Sixty-two years later and Hitler no more
Along with sixty million people and the Second World War
What was the point of all that pain
When at the end of the day there was nothing to gain?
The most terrible ending, from a terrible start
This man, Adolf Hitler, he had not a heart
He tried and he tried to get things his way
But no one really cared what he had to say
The one who caused madness, destruction and pain
Was indeed Adolf Hitler, Adolf the insane.

Cerys Perkins (14)
Ysgol Glan y Môr Comprehensive, Burry Port

Turning Point

When I was the bully, I pushed you around
You were the person who'd fall to the ground.
I turned others against you, you had three friends only,
I was the person who never got lonely.

There were so many of us, but only one of you,
That's what we thought, me and my 'crew',
That you couldn't defend yourself on your own,
That the few friends you did have would leave well alone.

But we were all surprised to see you pull through,
With a smile on your face as your confidence grew.
It was those three friends, who stuck by your side,
And helped you until you'd no longer hide.

After that we realised, that it was you with the strength,
You've proved your point and come a great length.
You're free at last to do as you please,
It's no longer you who's forced to their knees.

Now it's me that's always defeated,
With words so harsh, so wrongly treated.
My friends have turned on me, now they're the enemies
They've turned into the main bullies.

And yet, you stand by me, you've allowed us to be friends,
Now it's an honour, in the past an offence.
I've realised that you're a true friend,
You're helping me get my life on the mend.

Amy Beech (15)
Ysgol Glan y Môr Comprehensive, Burry Port

Dreams

When I grow up I want to be a pilot,
Flying planes
        Up and
            Down
Swooping and looping through the clouds.

When I grow up I want to be a superhero,
Fighting guys with my laser vision.
I'll blast them outta there
And into prison.

When I grow up I want to be a princess,
Wearing a tiara made of gold,
I'll be beautiful forever and never grow old.

When I grow up I want to be a policeman,
Firing at robbers with my very own gun
And eating doughnuts, sounds like fun.

When I grow up I want to be the prime minister,
I'll cut down taxes and stop global warming
So move over Blair,
Cos
      I'm
        Coming!

When I grow up I want to be an Olympic athlete,
I'll run like the wind, you can't stop me,
I'm gonna be the best runner the world's ever seen!

When I grow up I want to travel the world,
I'll visit Australia, America and Africa too.
I'll se crocodiles, pandas and kangaroos.

When I grow up I want to be just like my mam,
She hugs me when I'm down and she cuddles me when I'm sad.
She tells me things will be okay, when I know they're real bad.

When I grow up
        When I grow up
I want to be me.

Emily Downey (15)
Ysgol Glan y Môr Comprehensive, Burry Port

Rising

As the trees fall, the paper supply rises.
As the ice melts, the water rises.
As the sun sets, the moon rises.

As the trees fall, the paper supply rises.
As the roots are dug up,
As the branches are cut,
The leaves torn and ripped,
When it's all over,
The tree is left weeping silently,
Alone, torn, battered, a former image of itself.

As the ice melts, the water rises.
As the land disappears into the vast ocean
And rising rivers and swallowing swamps.
As the land is depleted,
The water is found searching for more
And more and more of the glorious landscape.

As the sun sets, the moon rises.
As the sun sets lowly casting a shadow across
The land, absorbing every last ray before it sets.
When the moon rises it harnesses the sun's rays
To give us a little light in the night.

As I watch all this happening in the world
I weep and hope that one day it will all go away.
As the trees fall, I weep,
As the ice melts, I weep,
As the sun sets, I weep,
Because I know that it will be a long time for another tree to grow,
And the ice will never stop melting as we heat the planet up,
And when the sun sets I know another day has been lost.
But sadly I realise this is my life, I must rise above it.

Aled Jones (15)
Ysgol Glan y Môr Comprehensive, Burry Port

Stand Up

As I gaze across the playground,
And look at the other side,
I see people in their element,
And some of their demise.

The image that most stands out to me
Is this little girl that I can see.

She sits at the picnic bench,
Without any friends.
Waiting for the moment
That this school day ends.

I pause for a moment,
And start to think,
'Why have I put her life on the brink?'

She used to be such a strong, happy girl,
Now at the first sign of fear,
She will straight away curl.
We have killed the person she used to be.
All my friends, my gang, and me.
I feel like such a murderer,
Why have I done this when, after all, I aspire to be her?

She is her own person,
She is unique,
Not following the crowds which are monotonous and bleak.

Beep! The buzzer goes,
This signals the end of the day,
I hear some sighs as some of the children
                    were enjoying their time of play.

I see a smile upon her face,
My friends look at her in disgrace.
'Let's get her,' they say and off they go,
I want to stand up for her and say to them, 'No!'

But it's too late, they've caught her, they start to kick and slap.
They grab her school bag and rip it off her back.

She starts to cry.
She pleads for them to stop,
I see a look in her eye and then her last teardrop.

She runs away,
Back to her home,
Which is very discreet and her address unknown.
My friends all laugh and walk away,
I can't see why we do this to her every day.

We come into school the next day,
All the children look our way.
Mrs Thomas comes out, 'I'd like to see you, please.'
The girls smile to try and put each other at ease.

'We've got some news about Melissa.
Last night she was found dead.'
Those two words that could have saved her were left unsaid.

A silent tear falls to my lap . . .
We had her like hungry vermin stuck in a mousetrap.

To this day I don't know why I lined up,
Waiting to hurt her when all I had to do was *stand up!*

Laura Richards (15)
Ysgol Glan y Môr Comprehensive, Burry Port

Perfect Family

It's mounted on the wall in a large, wooden frame,
My family and I all look the same.
Mum and dad either side of my sisters and I.
Every time I look at it, it makes me want to cry.

My family has changed now,
Mum and Dad together no more.
As time has gone by we've all grown apart
But they'll always be there in my heart.

Visitors can see as they walk in the door,
The picture of the *perfect family* that is no more.

Imogen Scutt (15)
Ysgol Glan y Môr Comprehensive, Burry Port

Why Don't You Care?

Why don't you care?

The grass is luscious
The sun is shining
Over a shimmering sea
What else in the world could there better be?

You fill the air
With pollution, unaware
Without thinking of the consequences
Or even stopping to care

Whales, tigers and elephants die
And in your warm beds you lie
Extinct, for your needs
Whilst at night they bleed

The oceans seem endless
But your tankers spill oil
Over the animals so helpless
On other nations' soils

So we ask ourselves why
There's a hole in the sky?
Whilst the ozone is damaged
And so is our planet

So stop asking why
And start asking how
For the world would repair
If only we cared.

Jenna Treharne (15)
Ysgol Glan y Môr Comprehensive, Burry Port

Green Or Mean

Saving our planet
Should be our top priority,
It is under threat
So it needs help from everybody.

I feel global warming
Is a real concern,
We should stop our wasting and throwing
Plus reduce the amount that we burn.

The Arctic's glaciers
Are in big trouble,
Because of the hole in the ozone layer
The temperature will surely double.

Floods, storms and heatwaves
Will happen more frequently,
We need our politicians to be brave
And act now to be more eco-friendly.

Be green and recycle
That's what we all need to do,
Use our cars less and cycle
Walking is good exercise too.

Tidal and solar power
Will keep our air clean,
We need to use less nuclear
To be green and not mean.

Rebecca Evans
Ysgol Glan y Môr Comprehensive, Burry Port

The Harsh Reality

Dozens more are killed in Iraq,
Terrorist organisation exclaims another warning,
Another loss of life at the hands of a murderer,
Another cold-blooded gun assassination,
Refugees flee war-torn country,
And this is just the news.
I turn off the television and pick up the newspaper.
Unsurprisingly, only to find more stories of suffering, despair
and anguish.

People starving, poverty,
Murders, deprived children,
War-torn countries, corrupt leaders,
What more?
Look out of the window,
And think of the pain and the suffering - it's out there somewhere.
As you stare at the food piled on your plate.
Think of them.
As you lay in your warm, comfortable bed tonight,
Think of them.
Who, you ask innocently?
You know who – the people you see on the TV,
The people who you see in books and on posters,
The people you are urged to help once every year.
These people know the harsh reality of life.
These people are not mere numbers or statistics on the news,
These people are real, just like you.
And some of these people died whilst you simply ate your food,
Whilst you simply watched the TV, whilst you sat, bored, in school.
This is the truth. This is the world, the cruel world that we live in.
This is the harsh reality of life.

James Thomas (14)
Ysgol Glan y Môr Comprehensive, Burry Port

Perception Of War

I am Emperor W Bush and I am here to rule the world
God of war, spurred on by greed and gore,
A search for oil is what I'm for, as I push the buttons of war.
I'll give a speech and I'll declare,
'It's for my country that I care!
Boys, get your guns and have some fun,
Stand tall, look sharp, pray to the sun.
Show me respect, though you'll earn none
And pretty soon, you'll be a man.
Destruction, death, that's what you'll see,
I'll lead you into World War III.'
As the world watches widows laying flowers,
He's off to Iraq - they killed his towers!
Whilst on our doorstep a military grows,
Nations from alliances, the truth they now know.
Where once there were children, with friends, having fun,
Now we see soldiers, stood tall with a gun.
Where once there was laughter, now we see dread,
They long to be safe, curled up warm in bed.
But around them the streets are polluted, stained red,
As childhood friends, relatives, now lay dead.
Have mercy on them, give them a chance, let them feed,
After all, it doesn't cost much to plant a few seeds.
I know that your false perception of peace,
Will soon become past mistakes that will repeat.
So while you're in bed, tucked up in your silk sheets,
Think of the innocent, alone on the street.

Ainsley Jones (15)
Ysgol Glan y Môr Comprehensive, Burry Port

Man Against Nature

The blue sky above our heads,
the rich green grass below our feet.
The sea, enjoyed by all and its powerful waves.
These are nature's creation.

Traffic rushing past, filling the air with the smell of petrol,
power stations, their chimneys belching out pollution.
The mass of concrete around which our lives are centred.
These are Man's creation.
Tell me which do you prefer?

The green countryside.
The black smoke.
Towering mountains overlooking valleys.
Skyscrapers overlooking the bleak cityscape.
Golden sand warming in the sun.
The sun glaring off a traffic jam.

The difference between these things is
often not noticed until one disappears.
It is almost possible to see the power
consuming monster slowly eat away at nature.

Christopher Goddard (14)
Ysgol Glan y Môr Comprehensive, Burry Port

Stop

Stop repeating yourself.
Stop.
Stop.
Stop!
The way you boast about the deeds you have done.
I've seen everything, the violence, the horrific abuse,
The verbal and physical actions that you lashed upon that innocent,
Defenceless little child.
Stop! With your twisted lies.
Stop.
Stop.
Stop!
For she has a frail mind,
With vivid thoughts concerning her current ongoings.
Her thoughts reminisce the good of her past.
Your lies are made up just to get her in trouble.
I know why you go to all this controversy, you're just plain jealous.
Halt your pathetic behaviour.
Stop.
Stop.
Stop!

Laurence Jôb (14)
Ysgol Glan y Môr Comprehensive, Burry Port

Wales

Wales is my country,
Wales is where I live,
Wales is such a great place
Because it has so much to give.

The fields are always green
And the landscape picturesque,
The people are so happy,
Because they're not trapped behind a desk.

A land full of culture,
It leaks out of every seam,
You can hear the songs and poems
From every valley to every stream.

People come from far and wide
To visit and to stay,
The children love to run along
Every beach and every bay.

The cuisine is so uplifting,
Laver bread, bara brith and cawl,
These foods are surely more than enough
To generate a smile from a scowl.

Some of the emblems of Wales
Are a daffodil or leek
And the flag is so unique,
It instills a sense of patriotism
Should you want to take a peek.

Wales is a land
Where folk are free to roam,
Wales is not just my country
Wales is my home.

Steven William Lewis (14)
Ysgol Glan y Môr Comprehensive, Burry Port

Answer Me This

Why am I the one,
That stands out from the crowd,
Yet . . . never included?

Why am I the one,
Being shunted from pillar to post,
When all I want is peace?

Why am I the one,
Dreaming of solidarity?

So why am I the one?

Life . . . or death?

It hangs in the balance!
You have the will to let me live,
But, haven't got the guts.

Why am I the one,
Who stands up for my opinions?

Why am I the one,
Trying to make a difference?

So why am I the one,
With scars as deep as trenches?

I'll tell you!

I am me!
I will fight!
I will stand up for what's right!
I will try and stop bullying!
I will get justice!   But,
I will . . . be me!

Life or revenge?
It's as clear as day,
There isn't a choice

I choose freedom   I choose life!

Stephen Sellers (15)
Ysgol Glan y Môr Comprehensive, Burry Port

Untitled

Teardrops fell down from my cheek,
As I looked at her body, so lifeless and weak.
To think I was the only one who was to blame,
The person who burnt her hair with a flame.

'You're fat and ugly,' are the words we used to taunt her every day,
Then later that night, she'd go home and pray
For all of this pushing and shoving to stop,
It really had gone over the top.

The torment continued, almost every lunchtime,
Little did I know I was committing a crime.

I was in school when I heard the news,
The victim was dead. Was it my fault?
I wouldn't refuse.

Now I'm finding it hard to live with this guilt.
Every night I silently cry under my quilt.
I am a bully. I lay in disgust.
Stand up for every victim I must.

I cannot believe I am responsible for this person's death.
Rest in peace, you didn't deserve it Beth.

Laura Davies (15)
Ysgol Glan y Môr Comprehensive, Burry Port

Global Warming

The effects of global warming are easy to see.
It's going on all around you and me.
Global warming isn't hard to explain,
It leaves Mother Nature crying with pain.

There are sure effects of global warming,
It means that this world is suddenly transforming.
Rainforests cut down, ice caps shrinking,
All of this happening, it's got me thinking.

We could save Mother Nature from being destroyed,
The way some people don't care really makes me annoyed.

If we all took the bus instead of the car,
There would less carbon monoxide in the air, this would really go far.
If we were all eco-friendly and we all went *green,*
Maybe our behaviour towards the environment wouldn't be so mean.

So next time you travel or throw litter on the floor,
Stop!
And think, *for the environment, I could do more.*

Sophie Hawkins (15)
Ysgol Glan y Môr Comprehensive, Burry Port

Relief

I can see the school now
I'm running through the gate
I can barely breathe and
I know that I am late

I come into the classroom
Trying to walk tall
The class burst into laughter
And I feel very small

I'm the butt of every joke
It is always me
I can't take it any longer
I know I must break free

I have to get through this
I need some self-belief
I need to find a better place
I must get some relief

I paint a pretty picture
I paint it with a twist
I paint it with a razor blade
I paint it on my wrist.

Rebekha Maskell (14)
Ysgol Glan y Môr Comprehensive, Burry Port

That Lonely Old Man

That lonely old man,
in his hospital bed,
had nobody to love,
so everyone said.

His grey, wispy hair,
his dark, hollow eyes,
his deep engraved wrinkles,
and his unloved sighs.

He sits there alone,
day after day,
no family to talk to,
as his life slips away.

That lonely old man.
left his hospital bed,
to dance with the angels,
so everyone said.

Ellie Pring (15)
Ysgol Glan y Môr Comprehensive, Burry Port

Another Day

Another day
I am alone
Another day
I am left
Another day
Abandoned
Another day
With no one
Another day
They see me
Another day
They watch me
Another day
They laugh at me
Another day
They hurt me
Another day
They lie

Another day
I wish I were somewhere else
Hoping
That one day
I'll have friends
I'll be the centre of attention
With everyone
They'll see me . . . happy
They'll watch me . . . playing
They'll laugh with me
They'll help me
They'll always tell me the truth

But another day
Another day
And another day passes
And I'm alone.

Howell Duggan (15)
Ysgol Glan y Môr Comprehensive, Burry Port

Dad's Home

It must be time
I've been waiting a long time
The light has gone dark,
I can hear the noises of children.
My owners must be home soon.
Hush, there's the noise of children,
I'll go to the window.
No, not this time.
I'll sit back in my bed.
I can't wait.
Oh, another car,
To the window I go.
Yes, yes, I can't stop wagging my tail.
It's my daddy.
I go back to my bed.
I get my bone.
Yes, yes, Daddy's home.
I hear the key in the door,
And I don't wait anymore,
I waggle my tail and bark, *Woof, Woof.*
And see my daddy coming
In from the dark.
Yes, I jump up and lick his face.
He pats my back.
Says I'm a good boy.
I go to basket to pick up my toy.
I'm happy now,
Because Daddy's home,
I'm a happy boy.

Kurt Frazer (12)
Ysgol-y-Gwendraeth, Llanelli

Life Through My Great-Grandmother's Eyes

As a child I used to play
In my home village called Carway.
I had a happy life with my mother and father,
My sister Meirwen and Brinley my brother.

I married Will and then soon after,
Along came Cynthia, my dear daughter.
I played my role throughout my life,
As a schoolgirl, a mother and a wife.

Things have now changed since I was younger,
With diseases like AIDS and countries with hunger.
Global warming is taking its toll,
With the ice caps melting 'cause of the ozone hole.

The wars are now never-ending,
With no signs of Iraq ever surrendering.
Innocent people getting killed,
And gallons of blood being spilled.

The TV has changed from black and white,
To coloured screen that's big and bright.
With satellite, Sky and LCD,
You can watch everything on your TV.

My granddaughter, Gail, whom I've looked after,
Is now herself an awesome mother.
Bringing up alone her two young sons,
She tells me, 'Gran, I love them tons.'

Children these days have mobile phones,
With coloured wallpapers and funky ringtones.
There were no such things when I was young,
But we still managed to have loads of fun.

Every night throughout the week,
We would play hopscotch or hide-and-seek.
No Playstation, Game Boys, snooker or pool,
If you don't own these now, you're so uncool!

As time has passed and years have flown,
My experience, knowledge and love has grown.
My health no longer as it used to be,
My ears don't hear and my eyes can't see.

I am now the proud age of ninety-two,
And there isn't much left that I can do.
I now sit in a nursing home, it's called Parcwern,
But soon I'll be there up in Heaven.

Alex Shaun Williams (11)
Ysgol-y-Gwendraeth, Llanelli

The World Of Spirits

You may not believe
But I know it's true.
When you die
It's only a mere pod
That is who dies.
Some spirits are human,
Some are older.
Some are violent and some are not.
In a room full of candles,
Full of peace,
Concentrate
And they will speak.
Ask yes/no questions,
Two knocks for yes
One for no.
They will answer
If you believe
That it is so.
Watch out or you'll be possessed.
It could be good
Or may be not nice.
You may not believe
But I *know* it's true.

Martin Denning (11)
Ysgol-y-Gwendraeth, Llanelli

Does Death Frighten You?

'Does death frighten you?'
The angel asked Rose,
'If it should hurt, then yes I suppose.

If I should die, then what would I see?
Would you be there to comfort me?'
'Yes,' said the angel, 'I shall show thee,
If you would like to follow me.

If you have been good, and well-behaved,
From the Devil you will be saved,
Follow me, but do not tell, for I will show you what lies in Hell.

This is where you will not go, for you've been good and that I know.
A death beholds you, that will be painless and calm,
And I will make sure you come to no harm.'

'Then why do you show me this kind of Hell,
As you yourself said, I've done well?'
'This is what happens if you do sin,
The Devil will be waiting to let you in.

Now I shall show you what lies in Heaven,
Count with me one to seven.
In this place your dreams will come true,
This is the path you should pursue.'

'I tell you my angel, I have no fear,
Knowing that I shall end up here.
For when I die, painless and calm,
I know for sure I will come to no harm.

But now that I've made a brand new friend,
I will see you in Heaven when my life comes to an end.'

Natalie Wheelhouse (11)
Ysgol-y-Gwendraeth, Llanelli

Australia

Australia, Australia,
What a wonderful place,
With the sun and sea
And surf.

Australia, Australia,
No rain. No clouds,
Not like in Wales!
Downpours and gales.

Australia, Australia,
My sister has just been,
She came back last year,
And she looked like a cocoa bean.

Australia, Australia,
What great memories I have,
The sun and the beaches,
They were all just fab.

Elin Cheedy (12)
Ysgol-y-Gwendraeth, Llanelli

Take A Walk

Take a walk to the army,
Maybe there's a dead person
Or a person trying to shoot you,
Or a bomb going off.

Take a walk to the army
Maybe you will see a head with one eye,
Or a man getting killed,
Or a woman getting run over.

Take a walk to the army,
Even if there's a mummy
Even if there's a devil.

Take a walk to the army,
At least you'll have some fun.

Keelan Evans (12)
Ysgol-y-Gwendraeth, Llanelli

The Girl Without A Voice

I am the girl, without a voice,
Hoping I would have a choice,
For you to hear me loud and clear,
And to banish all my inner fear.

I cannot speak my hopes and fears,
Instead I listen to my peers,
I'd love to laugh and sing and shout,
Instead my voice just won't come out.

I'd shout from the rooftops,
I'd shout from the stairs,
I'd shout with passion,
I'd shout everywhere.

Now you've heard my story,
You know I have no choice,
I'd like to talk to all my friends,
I am the girl, without a voice.

Brittany Hurlin (11)
Ysgol-y-Gwendraeth, Llanelli

The Dolphin

The dolphins sing
To the waves of the ocean,
Jumping up and down
With great emotion,
Looking up into the sky,
Wishing they could share their voice
With everyone around them.
They are different to fish.
They swim gracefully
And they think to themselves
People are cheering for me,
To be who I am,
And that's a dolphin.

Holly Lannigan (12)
Ysgol-y-Gwendraeth, Llanelli

Great Times - Llangranog

I have great memories of a time last year,
I went to Llangranog with primary,
I stayed in a room with five friends,
I had great fun and enjoyed all the time,
The first night was scary,
The fire alarm went off,
We ran outside in our pyjamas,
It was quite fun in the end,
There were a lot of activities during this time,
It was a great experience,
There was roller-blading, skiing, go-karting
And swimming.
It was pretty amazing,
Tobogganing was fun,
I went on with my friends,
I sped down the red slope,
Came to the end and started again.
Another one is horse riding,
Urgh! I didn't like that!
I sat on the horse and guess what?
I came off straight away.
On the last night there was a disco,
We all dressed up and went.
Everyone was dancing and singing,
And everyone was enjoying.
Then it came to the end,
We packed our things and got ready to go,
We waited outside for our bus.
We said goodbye to the friends we'd made,
Hoping to see them again.
Then we said goodbye to Llangranog.

Natalie Lloyd (11)
Ysgol-y-Gwendraeth, Llanelli

Hallowe'en

It's five o'clock
And it turns dark
The moon comes out
From behind the stars.

The children play
All dressed up
Then everyone says,
'It's six o'clock.'

They make their way
Around the street
And knock on doors
And say, 'Trick or treat?'

All they have
Are some sweets
But they don't mind
Because it's a treat.

Ghosts and skeletons
Can't come out
People think that they will pounce.

But we all know
That they don't exist
So enjoy
Hallowe'en kids!

Jessica Dunning (11)
Ysgol-y-Gwendraeth, Llanelli

Take A Walk

Take a walk to the moon,
Maybe there's an alien there,
A man,
Or a UFO.

Take a walk to the moon,
Maybe you'll see a spaceship
Or a jet
Or a rocket.

Take a walk to the moon,
Even if there's nobody there,
Even if there's nothing there.

Take a walk to the moon,
At least you fly into space.

Thomas Jones (12)
Ysgol-y-Gwendraeth, Llanelli

Take A Walk To Heaven

Take a walk to the light
Maybe there's your family
And pets
Or your best friend
Take a walk to the park
Maybe you'll see your best friend
Or family
Take a walk to the shop
Even if there are shoes
Even if there are clothes
Take a walk to Heaven
At least my mum and dad
Are there.

Deanna Jackson (13)
Ysgol-y-Gwendraeth, Llanelli

Wales, Grand Slam 2005

We beat England, Italy, France and Scotland in very hard games,
It was now the turn of Ireland who fight like Viking Danes.
We were playing in Cardiff, at the Millennium Stadium,
With a roaring crowd,
It was like opening night at the London Palladium.

On a bright March day, Owen led us out,
With our fans behind us a win was without a doubt.
Charlotte got us singing together with Boyce,
Everyone was ready with a proud voice.

Old Jenks the prop scored our first try,
He made such a good break it made Ireland cry.
With a Gavin penalty and drop goal,
We went in half-time with more luck than coal.

Kevin Morgan took us to 29-6,
And Jones converted the ball between the sticks.
The Irish went on to score two tries in the second half,
It made us worry. *Oh no, not 'alf.*

Jones had four penalties all together,
The second half seemed to last forever.
When the ref blew for full time,
The feeling of having won was sublime.

I picked up the cup the first time since 1978,
The nation was proud, we'll remember this date.
Me and my teammates could not stop grinning,
What a wonderful feeling was this feeling of winning!

James Stevenson (12)
Ysgol-y-Gwendraeth, Llanelli

Rugby

Rugby is the best sport, I cannot deny.
I don't recommend rugby if you are shy.
We pass the ball and kick it too,
And the forwards drive the ball on through.

We have scrums, lineouts and penalties too,
The ref makes decisions but not all true.
Boys racing for the try line,
Kicking up dirt,
But some boys get unlucky
And so they get hurt.

We run with the ball in our hands,
We hear at the sidelines all our fans,
But we hear someone shouting,
Louder than the rest.
It's our mums screaming . . .
'You are the best!'

Chris Morgan (12)
Ysgol-y-Gwendraeth, Llanelli

In Her Eyes

It's full of bees and broccoli trees,
Shooting stars and long limo cars.
Jelly pools and Hollywood schools.
Paris Hilton sailing on a cruise.

Lowri Tillman (11)
Ysgol-y-Gwendraeth, Llanelli

Young Writers Information

We hope you have enjoyed reading this book - and that you will continue to enjoy it in the coming years.

If you like reading and writing poetry drop us a line, or give us a call, and we'll send you a free information pack.

Alternatively if you would like to order further copies of this book or any of our other titles, then please give us a call or log onto our website at
www.youngwriters.co.uk

**Young Writers Information
Remus House
Coltsfoot Drive
Peterborough
PE2 9JX**

(01733) 890066